NEW MOCKTAILS BIBLE

All Occasion Guide to an Alcohol-Free, Zero-Proof, No-Regrets, Sober-Curious Lifestyle

ANNE SCHAEFFER

FOX CHAPEL
PUBLISHING

© 2022 by Fox Chapel Publishing Company, Inc., 903 Square Street, Mount Joy, PA 17552.

New Mocktails Bible is a compilation of new contributed recipes and photographs and selected recipes and photographs from various IMM publications and also from *Growing Your Own Tea Garden*, CompanionHouse Books, an imprint of Fox Chapel Publishing [2019]; and *Growing Your Own Cocktails, Mocktails, Teas & Infusions*, CompanionHouse Books, an imprint of Fox Chapel Publishing [2020].

Recipe selection, design, and book design © Fox Chapel Publishing.
Unless otherwise noted, recipes and photographs pages 34–69 © their respective contributors; photographs pages 12–17 by David Fisk.

ISBN 978-1-4971-0327-6

Library of Congress Control Number: 2022934219

To learn more about the other great books from Fox Chapel Publishing, or to find a retailer near you, call toll-free 800-457-9112 or visit us at www.FoxChapelPublishing.com.

We are always looking for talented authors. To submit an idea, please send a brief inquiry to acquisitions@foxchapelpublishing.com.

Printed in China
First printing

Because working with cooking utensils, heat, and other materials inherently includes the risk of injury and damage, this book cannot guarantee that creating the recipes in this book is safe for everyone. For this reason, this book is sold without warranties or guarantees of any kind, expressed or implied, and the publisher and the author disclaim any liability for any injuries, losses, or damages caused in any way by the content of this book or the reader's use of the tools needed to complete the recipes presented here. The publisher and the author urge all readers to thoroughly review each recipe and to understand the use of all tools before beginning any recipe.

The following images are from Shutterstock.com: Front cover, 1 top middle left, 10 bottom left, 29 bottom right: New Africa; front cover, 1 top middle right: Shebeko; front cover main image: smspsy; front cover bottom left: G.MARTYSHEVA; front cover, 1 top left and top right, back cover top: Serhiy Shullye; drink icons on spine and throughout: RedKoala; endpapers, 2, 202: M.Stasy; 3, 149 bottom: 5PH; 5: Evgeny Karandaev; 11 bottom left, 155 and 174 top, 171 top, 175 bottom: Africa Studio; 14 wood grain: Guiyuan Chen; 17 bottom: Mariyana M; 23: slowmotiongli; 24 right: bonchan; 26: Dirk Ott; 27 top: Nadiasantoso; 27 bottom: sjk2012; 28: marekuliasz; 29 top left: Maks Narodenko; 29 bottom left: oksana2010; 29 top right: Nattika; 61: SrideeStudio; 86: Angelina Zinovieva; 94: Brent Hofacker; 117: Wuttichok Panichiwarapun; 131, 135 bottom: Goskova Tatiana; 144 top, 175 top: Heike Rau; 147 bottom: Madeleine Steinbach; 150 top: Alexey Lysenko; 151 bottom: MarieKaz; 172: Irina Burakova; 173 top: Kasabutskaya Nataliya; 174 bottom: ILEISH ANNA; 176 top: Snowbelle; 177 top: LianeM; 194: Carey Jaman

Contents

Welcome to the New Era of Great Drink Experiences!

It may surprise you to learn that I really can't stand what the word "mocktail" used to mean—the old super-sweet concoctions made only with sweetened sodas, juices, syrups, and purées. At Mocktail Beverages, we are thrilled to be stretching the limits of what is possible with our head mixologist Ezra Star and our team of very talented people, and we are equally thrilled to be among the first businesses bringing this new industry to life. We stand in good company, as evidenced by some of the amazing drinks in the pages ahead.

It may also surprise you that I and many of our employees do drink alcohol. I enjoy a cocktail before dining out, a glass of wine occasionally with dinner, or a beer just because it hits the spot. I enjoy the experience and the taste of alcohol, and, while I did overdo it a bit when I was young, I never felt like I was addicted. I had fun, loved the wine tours and cocktail parties, and have great memories of business outings and events with family and friends. All that is to say—nothing we do is against alcohol because many of us are drinkers, too. We are flexitarians, moderates, and innovators that stand for a healthy lifestyle and the beliefs that great food and drinks with family and friends adds to the quality of life and that moderation is essential in all areas of life.

Even just ten years ago uttering the phrase "I'm not drinking tonight" at a social event could create so many questions and so much awkwardness that many people often chose to avoid the subject altogether by simply not going out. Anyone not drinking in the past suffered through the "less than great" experience of being limited to water, soda, or iced tea while it felt like everyone else in the room enjoyed a craft beer or inventive cocktail. The questions from others were often uncomfortable or downright invasive: are you okay, are you on medication, are you pregnant, etc. Most people trying to avoid alcohol or even just drink less of it felt alone and separated at many social occasions.

Not only are we not alone, but we're the vast majority! These types of stories have been repeated often as people have started to publicly share their common need for better, more inclusive ways to be social. Still today, however, 99% of all hospitality locations include only soft drinks, iced tea, or super-sweet juice mixes on their menus. *WHY* is this change so difficult?

We must remember that throughout human history and across many cultures, it has been important to bond over the traditions of breaking bread and sharing drinks. Feasts and celebrations of all sorts for centuries included alcohol and when people gather in modern times to celebrate, break bread, bond, and get to know each other, it still includes alcohol and always will. But the world is evolving and will continue to do so for years to come. More and more people are realizing that athletes, designated drivers, those who are pregnant, those on medications, members of certain religions, people in substance abuse recovery, and those simply choosing not to drink alcohol for any number of reasons need to be included in these important community events. From a business perspective, we believe that we are "doing well by doing good"—it makes good business sense and is the right thing to do to provide everyone with a worthy drink experience and not separate people based on whether alcohol is in their glass.

Moderation is normal and many are seeking helpful guides to aid their moderation. This book is a recipe collection, but it can also be used as a pathway to bring people together so everyone can enjoy the party. The pages ahead will help to extend the movement beyond a few talented mixologists to the millions of people at home looking for ways to re-engage with guests and serve drinks that are equally delicious and inspired whether they are alcoholic or not. Enjoy the incredible cocktails in the pages to follow!

Bill Gamelli

Founder and CEO
Mocktail Beverages, Inc.

Introduction

We all know there are many good reasons to enjoy alcohol-free drinks. Whatever your reasons, this book offers you a wide range of alcohol-free cocktail recipes to provide a delightful drinking experience that's accessible to everyone.

Along with the recipes, this book guides you through NA cocktail mixing from start to finish. The Equipment section on page 8 lists all the kitchen and bar tools you might need to become a master mixologist. Journalist Suzan Eraslan gets you started with stocking your home bar on page 12 and Douglas Watters, the founder of New York's first booze-free bottle shop, explores some of the available NA spirit flavors, comparing them to their alcoholic cousins. A well-stocked bar doesn't only include the alcohol-free alternatives, however, so the Other Handy Ingredients for Your Bar section on page 23 explores all the extras you can use to elevate your cocktails. Once your kitchen and bar are stocked, you're ready to start mixing, and Club Soda founder Laura Willoughby MBE walks you through mixing the perfect NA drinks at home on page 30. Finally, use the Glossary on page 32 to make sure you truly know the lingo and can mix and order NA cocktails with confidence.

Remember, alcohol-free cocktails, also known as "virgin" drinks or "mocktails," don't have to be boring. A clever bartender knows how to blend flavors to create exciting drinks, whether they are intoxicating or not. It's all about creating a balance: sweet with sour, savory with fruity—the combinations are endless. Begin with the recipes in this book, and as you get comfortable, try mixing new flavors and ingredients to create your own signature cocktails!

> **NOTE:** this book offers a range of recipes that provide approximate quantities or proportional quantities for each ingredient. No matter the measurements used in your country or whether you're serving a single drink or mixing for a crowd, these recipes should give you the basics you need. The recipes also work as guidelines that you can alter, adjust, and experiment with to suit your own tastes.

Try this refreshing Grecian Lady. Recipe on page 109.

Equipment

Whether you find your pleasure in skydiving, golf, jogging, or mixing drinks, you'll need some basic equipment to get you started. It's not always necessary to surround yourself with all the latest hi-tech gizmos—unless you are a full-time professional—but a few basic tools will increase your enjoyment and make things easier. Stores that stock bar supplies will offer you all manner of blenders, shakers, strainers, squeezers, and crushers, all of which are fun to use. But for an occasional party with friends, a few simple tools you may already have in your kitchen should do the trick.

CHOPPING BOARD
This comes in handy for cutting fruit for your drinks. A wooden board makes cutting easy and protects the knife blade and your work surface.

BAR KNIFE
Any smallish, very sharp knife will do here. You'll find it handy for cutting neat slices of lemon, dicing fruit, and slitting the foil on bottle necks.

JIGGER
It's handy to have a jigger (also known as a bar measure) available to make it easier to pour consistent quantities. Probably the most useful measure is one with two cups fixed bottom to bottom and fitted with a handle. Alternatively, you can use a shot glass or egg cup.

COCKTAIL SHAKER
Useful for blending ingredients, particularly those of different consistencies, like cream and fruit juice. A few cubes of ice inside act as beaters and slightly dilute the ingredients. Cocktail shakers are usually fitted with strainers, so you can pour the drink while keeping the ice cubes behind.

BLENDER
This is a valuable piece of bar equipment that makes nice smooth milkshakes and can be used to turn soft fruits like bananas and peaches into a creamy purée in a few seconds. It's worth investing in one because you'll find plenty of uses for it in your kitchen.

Cocktail shakers are indispensable bar tools for mixing and straining ingredients.

A blender is always useful in the kitchen, and it's a must-have for mixing creamy drinks.

An ice bucket and tongs is an elegant way to keep ice at the ready for your guests.

ICE BUCKET AND TONGS
Almost all mocktails call for ice in one form or another. You could always use a mixing bowl from the kitchen, of course, but an ice bucket keeps the ice cold and looks good on the bar.

ICE CRUSHER
Many drinks call for crushed ice, so if you're going to be reasonably serious about your mocktails, a manual or electric ice crusher is a great help. The alternative is to place ice cubes in a bag or linen tea towel and smack them with a meat tenderizing hammer. Some hosts prefer to whack the ice bag against a wall to crush the ice. A little dramatic and inelegant, but it does work!

ASSORTED JUGS, PITCHERS, AND BOWLS
You need a selection of bowls, jugs, and pitchers (preferably with ice guards) to store supplies of iced water, fruit juices, milk, and cream. You don't want to have to rush out to the kitchen every time you need another glass of water.

The shape and size of your glass can affect the flavor of the drink and will definitely affect the visual appeal.

Adding a sugar or salt rim to your drink is an easy way to both amp up your flavor combinations and elevate your presentation.

Handheld frothers are best known for their use in creating foamy toppings for coffee drinks, but they can be used to aerate and add texture to your mixed drinks, as well.

GLASSES

Mocktail recipes often call for particular types of glasses—highball glasses, lowball glasses, martini glasses, champagne flutes, wine glasses, and so on. It's really not necessary to have them all, unless you're running a professional bar. You'll get by perfectly well with a selection consisting of wine glasses, tall cylindrical glasses, and shorter rocks glasses. If you do become more serious, the traditional martini glass is an attractive addition. For short drinks or "shooters" you could add a few shot glasses to your collection.

RIMMED GLASSES

Some drinks call for rimmed glasses. To achieve this, have a saucer of caster sugar handy, run a slice of lemon or orange around the rim of the glass to moisten it, then dip it into the saucer so that the sugar sticks to the damp rim. See How to Make Caster Sugar, page 23. In the case of savory drinks, salt can be used instead of sugar and the rim dampened with one of the drink's ingredients instead of lemon juice. If you plan to serve a few drinks in rimmed glasses, they can be prepared in advance and stored in the refrigerator. The more preparation a good host does ahead of the party, the less stressful the event will be. And ideally, the host should have as much fun as the guests!

FROTHER

Handheld frothers, small slim gadgets similar to immersion blenders, can be used to aerate milk or cream to create foamy toppings for coffee drinks, but can also be used to add foam and texture to your cocktails and other mixed drinks. Frothing the ingredients can be an alternative for those drinks that normally create foam using an egg or egg white.

A small grater will help you add the small professional touches, like a dusting of fresh nutmeg or cinnamon, that can make all the difference.

Cocktail sticks or toothpicks , whether plain or decorated, are useful for keeping garnishes tidy.

Vegetable peelers can be useful bar tools, making it easy to peel thin strips of citrus zest for aroma and visual interest.

TEA TOWELS OR KITCHEN TOWELS

No matter how tidy you are, serving drinks can be a damp activity. Have a few small, clean tea towels or kitchen towels handy to mop up spills and dry hands and glasses.

STIRRING SPOON

A slim, long-handled bar spoon is good to have around. It reaches right to the bottom of tall glasses, jugs, or pitchers for mess-free stirring.

GRATER

This is not a must, but it does add a touch of professionalism. A small grater can be useful for grating fresh nutmeg or for grating chocolate over coffee or dessert drinks.

COCKTAIL STICKS OR TOOTHPICKS

Many drinks call for a cherry or olive as a garnish. You can spear these on ordinary wooden toothpicks or use special party cocktail sticks sometimes decorated with frilly tops, flags, umbrellas, or figurines.

VEGETABLE PEELER

You probably have one of these already. It's handy for peeling thin strips of lemon or orange zest from the fruit. If you're going to be serious about virgin cocktails, it's also worth buying a zester, which takes very neat, thin strips of zest from the skin of an orange or lemon.

Stocking Your Alcohol-Free Bar: A Buyer's Guide

CONTRIBUTED BY SUZAN ERASLAN, PROMINENT JOURNALIST AND NON-ALCOHOLIC MIXOLOGIST

Once you're outfitted with the right tools, it's time to stock your bar. The pleasure derived from mocktails comes exclusively from taste, and since you can't hide mediocre flavors behind the sensory-blurring effects of alcohol, using the best-tasting ingredients is even more important than in traditional bartending. With the explosion of non-alcoholic options over the last few years, it can be overwhelming (and expensive) to try everything on the market, so I've compiled a practical guide to help you get started! *(Note: all product names, trademarks, and registered trademarks mentioned on the following pages are property of their respective owners.)*

Non-alcoholic Base Spirits

A well-stocked non-alcoholic bar begins with five basic spirits: gin, whiskey, rum, tequila, and vodka. While some NA spirits, particularly apéritifs and digestifs, are distilled from ingredients like herbs, spices, and botanicals that are listed on the label, almost all base spirits are a combination of water, glycerin, and natural flavors. This makes it impossible to identify by label alone which liquor alternatives taste most like the real thing, but I've tasted dozens, and I recommend the following:

GIN: Monday Zero Alcohol Gin has a classic, strong juniper-forward flavor that is a spot-on imitation of a top shelf London Dry. Stock it alongside Lyre's Apéritif Dry (a dry vermouth alternative) for perfect martinis, top with a good quality tonic water for a refreshing hot-weather highball, or add fresh-squeezed lemon juice, simple syrup, and non-alcoholic sparkling wine for a French 75.

WHISKEY: Spiritless Kentucky 74's oaky bourbon flavor works beautifully for a whiskey highball with cola or ginger ale, an old fashioned, or a Manhattan with Lyre's Apéritif Rosso. If you're a whiskey enthusiast who knows their rye and sour mash from their bourbon and wants to mix accordingly, add a bottle of fiery Monday Zero Alcohol Whiskey for use in rye cocktails and some Free Spirits Spirit of Bourbon which, despite its name, makes a great Jack Daniels or Southern Comfort substitute when mixed with lemonade, ginger ale, and cola.

RUM: For mojitos, daiquiris, and other clear or white rum drinks, the straightforward sugarcane flavor of Lyre's White Cane Spirit performs beautifully. If you're making Cuba Libres, rum old fashioneds, and creamy flips like eggnog, opt for the rich, caramel flavor of darker Ritual Zero Proof Rum.

VODKA: Though sold as a gin alternative, I find that the subtle flavor and pronounced burn of Free Spirits Spirit of Gin is the best substitute for vodka in cosmos, cranberry juice, and even martinis.

TEQUILA: Either of Lyre's tequila alternatives (Agave Blanco Spirit and Agave Reserva Spirit) will work perfectly in tequila drinks like margaritas and palomas, or in a simple tequila and tonic. Agave Blanco Spirit is like a light, silver tequila, and Agave Reserva Spirit is more like a gold or reposado tequila; choose whichever you prefer. Though not as versatile as the refined and filtered flavor of tequila, if you're looking for a hefty, savory, and smoky mezcal alternative, try Harmony Smoked Apéritif.

Liqueurs, Apéritifs, and Digestifs

To expand your mocktail-making horizons beyond the simple rum-and-coke– or gin-and-tonic–style highball, you'll need non-alcoholic liqueurs, apéritifs, and digestifs to punch up the flavor and complexity of your drinks.

As mentioned above, Lyre's makes the most accurate versions of vermouth, both dry (Apéritif Dry) and sweet (Apéritif Rosso), and their impressions of Campari (Italian Orange), Aperol (Italian Spritz), and Absinthe are all worth stocking for spritzes and spirit-forward cocktails like negronis, martinis, and Sazeracs. For triple sec, I prefer Sexy AF's Triple Sexy over Lyre's Orange Sec; it has a richer mouthfeel that stands up to the large volume of lime juice and simple syrup in a margarita; and it gives a luxurious weight to cosmopolitans.

A non-alcoholic amaro (a bitter, aromatic, herbal liqueur) adds wonderful sophistication to zero-proof cocktails and can be enjoyed sipped on its own as an after-dinner digestif. For exquisitely complex non-alcoholic amari, look for labels that include specific herbs, spices, and botanicals listed among the ingredients, rather than just "natural flavors." Few of these are easy to use as substitutes for specific brands of alcoholic amari, however, and will require some experimentation to find their best use in cocktail recipes. Collecting and tasting them can be an entirely enjoyable hobby in and of itself. A couple that can be reliably substituted one-for-one are Harmony Alpine Digestif, which is a perfect zero-proof replacement for Fernet-Branca; and Sexy AF Amar-Oh, a general-purpose workhorse that can step in for most warmly spiced, caramel-rich amari, like Meletti and Cardamaro.

Mixers and Juices

Because mocktails can't hide behind the psychotropic effects of alcohol, using good mixers and juices when making them is non-negotiable. Bottled mixers that use real cane sugar or natural sweeteners like agave nectar taste infinitely better than those that use high-fructose corn syrup or artificial sweeteners. Soda water, tonic, ginger ale, ginger beer, and cola are the conventional must-haves, though I encourage everyone to have one or two more adventurous flavors like AVEC Hibiscus and Pomegranate or Fever-Tree Sparkling Lime and Yuzu on hand, as well. Aways fresh squeeze your citrus juices, and, if you must buy bottled juices, get the highest quality with the fewest ingredients you can find. The only ingredient should be the fruit juice itself, or, in the case of cranberry juice, cranberry and a bit of sugar.

Syrups and Cordials

Flavored syrups and citrus cordials are a great way to add intense bursts of flavor to your mocktails without the extra volume of juices and sodas. Avoid coffee shop syrups like the kind used for flavored lattes and Italian sodas, as they are chock-

full of corn syrup and taste noticeably artificial in non-alcoholic cocktails. Look for syrups and cordials specifically made for cocktails (check labels to make sure they are alcohol-free) and always opt for those made with cane sugar, agave, or honey and real fruits, flowers, nuts, and spices rather than natural or artificial flavorings. I'm especially partial to gum or gomme syrups, like those made by Liber & Co., which add much-needed heft and the smooth, viscous mouthfeel of a real cocktail to non-alcoholic drinks—look for "gum arabic" or "acacia gum" among the listed ingredients.

Bitters

A dash of bitters is often *the* critical ingredient to tame the cacophony of spirits, juices, and mixers into a well-blended and balanced symphony of flavors. While a few drops of alcoholic bitters will not raise the alcohol by volume (ABV) of an otherwise non-alcoholic cocktail any higher than a glass of orange juice, there are now excellent zero-alcohol options for those who want to keep alcoholic ingredients out of their drinks altogether. For the obligatory Angostura, Peychaud's, and orange bitters, try All the Bitter Alcohol-Free Aromatic Bitters, New Orleans Bitters, and Orange Bitters. For options beyond the classics, DRAM Apothecary makes entirely alcohol-free bitters with unusual flavors like woodsy, sweet Palo Santo and calming Lavender Lemon Balm. There are other companies offering non-alcoholic bitters with glycerin or syrup bases, though I generally don't recommend them, as they often require heaping teaspoonfuls or even entire ounces to impart their flavor, which dramatically sweetens the drink. Adjust any syrups or other sweet ingredients accordingly if you decide to use them.

Beer

No longer deserving of its once dismal reputation, non-alcoholic beer has really come into its own in the last few years. Not just standard lagers, but hoppy IPAs, chocolatey stouts, and even unusual varieties like goses, weisses, and sours are now available to satisfy every type of beer lover. In general, avoid offerings by the giant brewing companies and stick to small, craft beer brewers, preferably those who exclusively make non-alcoholic beer, like Bravus Brewing Co., or my favorite, Athletic Brewing Co.

Wine

A truly great de-alcoholized wine is, in many ways, still the holy grail of non-alcoholic drinks. As of this writing, wine makers are actively experimenting with new technologies to remove the alcohol from wine without removing its flavor, but despite many claiming to have found the way to do it, in my opinion, they still have a long way to go. Alcohol-removed wine often tastes like grocery store grape juice, and to add insult to injury, costs wine shop prices! Instead, seek out wine alternatives like NON, Jukes Cordialities, and the dazzlingly complex Proxies by Acid League, which are all more flavorful, more exciting, and far more satisfying to the palate, and avoid de-alcoholized wine altogether. The one exception is sparkling wine; alcohol-removed bubblies by big commercial wine producers, like Freixenet's or Fre by Sutter Home, offer the crisp, dry, grown-up taste you want from blanc de blancs and rosés.

A Sampling of NA Spirits

CONTRIBUTED BY DOUGLAS WATTERS, FOUNDER OF SPIRITED AWAY, NEW YORK'S FIRST BOOZE-FREE BOTTLE SHOP.

Two years ago, an NA spirits guide covering ten products would have given the reader a reasonably good sense of the breadth of the space. Today, it merely scratches the surface. When my store opened in 2020, I sold about 30 different SKUs. Today, I have over 225 and I'm adding new ones every week. There isn't enough space here to list the many fine NA spirits that warrant mention, but this is a good starting point for your own research and taste adventures.

	WHISKEY ALTERNATIVES	
Name	**Spiritless Kentucky 74**	**Gnista Barreled Oak**
Description	Whereas most NA whiskey alternatives combine or conflate the flavors of different types of alcoholic whiskeys (Irish, Scotch, Tennessee, etc.), Spiritless's Kentucky 74 is one of the very few bourbon-specific NA whiskey alternatives.	A meatless burger patty can convincingly replace a meat burger patty when served on a toasted bun with cheese, mustard, and a pickle. Similarly, most NA whiskey alternatives are best enjoyed in a cocktail with a mixer, bitters, and a garnish. Gnista Barreled Oak, however, has body, mouthfeel, and burn that makes it very enjoyable neat or on the rocks.
Flavor Notes	Caramel, vanilla, charred oak, malty sweetness, smoke, and a hint of spice	Dry and smoky, with chocolate rye, warm spices and oak barrel
Notable Features	Vegan, gluten-free, keto-friendly, women-owned	Crafted by hand in small batches in Sweden
Notable Ingredients	Only 1g of sugar per serving	Dried spices and fruits, habanero extract, botanical distillates. Rhubarb juice and beet syrup for mouthfeel and body.
Comparable Alcoholic Spirits	Maker's Mark, Buffalo Trace, Town Branch	Old Forester, Four Roses, Wild Turkey
Mixing Suggestions	Best for Old Fashioneds and Whiskey Sours, but holds its own on the rocks or even neat	Best on the rocks or neat, but also works well with soda water and a maraschino cherry

Name	Mockingbird	Ritual Zero Proof	Free Spirits
Description	Mockingbird can't technically call itself a tequila since it's non-alcoholic, but it is made with tequila's traditional blue agave.	Ritual Zero Proof distinguishes itself by offering quality spirit alternatives at approachable prices. Their four spirits are widely available and a great place for NA cocktail newbies to start.	Somewhere in between the subtlety and nuance of Mockingbird and the bold spice of Ritual sits Free Spirits's tequila alternative, which they call The Spirit of Tequila.
Flavor Notes	Delicately earthy with floral vanilla and just a subtle hint of spice and smoke	Bold and spicy with agave, lime, guava, smoky mesquite, habanero	Agave with slight acidity and noticeable green bell pepper. Balanced sweetness and burn.
Notable Features	Mockingbird's blue Weber agave comes directly from Tequila, Mexico	I suspect the capsaicin in the habanero is what effectively mimics the slow burn of an alcoholic spirit.	Infused with B vitamins and amino acids like taurine to elevate mood, energy, and social experience
Notable Ingredients	Includes the adaptogen ashwagandha, a medicinal herb traditionally used to help the body manage stress and anxiety.	<1 g of sugar per serving	Fruit and vegetable juice, which I expect helps with mouthfeel and body as well as the subtle amber color
Comparable Alcoholic Spirits	Avion Anejo, Código 1530 Rosa Blanco, Mijenta Blanco	Jose Cuervo, Cazadores Reposado, Espolòn Reposado	Corralejo Reposado, Patrón Reposado, Camarena Reposado
Mixing Suggestions	Best for ranch water cocktails but also works well with St. Germain or an NA elderflower syrup	Best for big, bold, spicy, classic margaritas	Versatile and can be used for tequila and mezcal cocktails alike, including palomas. Makes an excellent Naked and Famous cocktail.

GIN ALTERNATIVES

Name	Monday	New London Light
Description	I always encourage people who are first exploring NA spirits not to limit themselves by their preferences for alcoholic spirits. Whether or not one likes alcoholic gins, most find that juniper, botanicals, and citrus flavors lend themselves naturally to NA spirits. Monday was one of the first and remains today one of the best premium NA gin alternatives.	Whereas the first non-alcoholic spirits came from new companies dedicated exclusively to NA, distilleries of alcoholic spirits have begun to produce NA offerings as well. South Devon, England's Salcombe Distilling Co. launched a luxury gin in 2016 and more recently put that expertise to use in crafting an NA London dry gin every bit as delicious as their leaded offering.
Flavor Notes	Citrus-forward. Bold yet balanced juniper, botanicals, and spices with a hint of cucumber	Fresh, complex, and herbaceous with orange, cardamom, and sage
Notable Features	Handmade in small batches in a Southern California distillery	Brand is heavily influenced by their coastal geography and gives one percent of profits to ocean sustainability initiatives
Notable Ingredients	Contains a small amount of monk fruit for a very slight sweetness that carries the botanical flavors without adding calories	Natural botanical distillates and extracts led by Macedonian juniper berries, ginger, and habanero capsicum
Comparable Alcoholic Spirits	Aviation, Tanqueray Rangpur, St. George Terroir Gin	Salcombe Start Point, Hayman's, Sipsmith London Dry
Mixing Suggestions	Best for gin an tonics with fresh lime and in other herbal, citrus-forward cocktails	Works well with an elderflower tonic water or with ginger beer

	DISTILLED BOTANICALS		
Name	Pentire Adrift	Seedlip Garden 108	Optimist Bright
Description	A difficult NA spirit to classify, Pentire's Adrift is the most juniper-forward of the distilled botanicals and thus could be mistaken for a gin, although its creators don't explicitly call it one.	Seedlip wisely chose to create complex spirits that can be enjoyed by lovers of both gin and vodka.	Bright is Optimist's citrus offering, showcasing a different flavor element that can be possible in botanicals.
Flavor Notes	Like an herbal gin with unique local botanicals foraged from Cornwall's surrounding headland	Fresh like a walk through an English garden in spring	Bright like lemon, jasmine, green mandarin, fennel, and cinnamon
Notable Features	A terroir NA spirit founded by environmentally conscious surfers and outdoorsmen, Pentire transports the drinker to the Cornish coast of the UK	Seedlip was the world's first NA spirit and inspired others to create novel botanical spirits, both NA and alcoholic.	Inspired by the diverse cultures of Los Angeles, Optimist dedicates 2% of its sales to providing access to mental health services for underserved youth.
Notable Ingredients	Rock samphire, sage, Pentire plant blend, citrus, and Cornish sea salt	Fresh, herbal blend of peas, hay, and traditional garden herbs including rosemary, thyme, and spearmint	Distillates and extracts of lemon, jasmine, green mandarin, lavender, turmeric, cornmint, orange, tangerine, fennel, myrrh, and cinnamon leaf
Comparable Alcoholic Spirits	Lantic Gin, Mermaid Gin, Dà Mhìle Seaweed Gin, Greenwich Marine London Dry	Ketel One Botanicals Cucumber & Mint, Grey Goose Essences Watermelon & Basil, Hendricks Midsummer Solstice	Ketel One Botanicals Grapefruit & Rose, Grey Goose Essences Strawberry & Lemongrass, Malfy Gin con Limone
Mixing Suggestions	Best with Indian tonic water and lime or a sprig of rosemary, or with flavored tonics like cucumber or elderflower	Seedlip has a strong scent, but a subtle flavor. Use a mixer with sugar to release the flavors, such as a good tonic water.	Same as Seedlip, best with tonic water and a citrus garnish

RUM ALTERNATIVES

Name	ISH RumISH	Caleño Dark & Spicy
Description	Dark spirits tend to be among the most challenging alcoholic drinks to replicate in a non-alcoholic alternative. ISH's RumISH from Copenhagen is leading the charge. They have created a crowd-pleasing NA spirit that everyone on my team at Spirited Away loves.	A bad experience as a younger drinker left me unable to stomach dark rums. I've always been jealous when friends ordered tropical drinks with colorful umbrellas and sunny beach vibes. One surprising discovery from early in my NA journey is that despite still to this day disliking traditional rums, I actually really like NA rums (and I love Caleño's Dark & Spicy)! Finally, I can join the tropical drinks party.
Flavor Notes	Rich and warm with notes of vanilla, caramel, nutmeg, and baked apple	Spicy and tropical with prominent pineapple and coconut, then vanilla, ginger, cardamom, and kola nut
Notable Features	An award-winning Danish company founded on the desire to introduce mindfulness into drinking by way of natural ingredients and familiar flavors	A British brand from a founder with Colombian heritage that inspired her to bottle the flavors, colors, and experiences of her family's homeland
Notable Ingredients	Vegetable glycerin adds body, mouthfeel, and a subtle, pleasant sweetness	Zero sugar, vegan, gluten-free
Comparable Alcoholic Spirits	Don Q Oak Barrel, Bounty Spiced Rum, Sailor Jerry	Gosling's Black Seal, Kōloa Kauai Coconut Rum, Mount Gay Eclipse
Mixing Suggestions	Great with ginger beer and lime in a Dark & Stormy, but best in an espresso martini: two parts each espresso and RumISH, one part Lyre's Coffee Originale, and an optional but recommended third part hazelnut syrup	Great in any tiki drink, umbrella drink, or boat drink. Also great in a simple Dark & Stormy with ginger beer and fresh lime.

Other Handy Ingredients for Your Bar

Unless yours is a professional bar, you can't be expected to stock every available ingredient used in mocktails. Rather, keep a few basic ingredients on hand so you can balance sweet with sour and bitter, and savory with fruit. The following list is just a suggestion and should enable you to create a good range of different drinks. Keep an eye open in supermarkets for interesting fruit syrups or toppings. It's amazing what you can use to create exciting drink experiences.

CASTER SUGAR
This fine white sugar, often used in baking, is ideal for sweetening drinks because it dissolves more easily than granulated sugar.

How to Make Caster Sugar

Caster sugar is a type of fine granulated sugar that's common in the United Kingdom. The texture falls somewhere between granulated sugar and confectioners' sugar. For those in the United States who might have trouble finding caster sugar, granulated sugar can often be used as a substitute (confectioners' sugar can never be used in place of caster sugar), but the best option is homemade caster sugar. To DIY your own caster sugar, pulse or blend granulated sugar in a

food processor, blender, or coffee grinder until it has a finely ground, but not powdery, texture (two or three quick pulses). Voilà!

Glacé or candied cherries are standard drink garnishes that add glossy color and a bit of sweetness.

COCKTAIL CHERRIES

Maraschino cherries are sweet and have a bright red, glossy shine. Glacé or candied cherries are Maraschino cherries that have been soaked in sugar syrup until the sugar replaces the moisture. Amarena cherries are a sweetly sour alternative. Cocktail cherries can sometimes be preserved in alcohol, so read labels carefully.

EGG

While some drinkers shudder at the thought of swallowing raw egg, it can add a delicious texture to any cocktail. Egg yolk gives a drink a velvet creaminess, while the white of an egg, shaken into a drink, lends it a silvery sheen that's very pretty. Eggs should be as fresh as they come and drinks containing raw egg yolk or egg white should be avoided by pregnant women and the elderly.

FRUIT PURÉE

Very useful to have when you're making cocktails, and easy to make in a blender. Simply place bananas, strawberries, ripe peaches, or watermelon chunks in the blender and whiz them to a smooth, creamy consistency. Fruit should be peeled, and any hard stones or pips should be removed before blending.

FRUIT SLICES

Fruit slices, especially citrus, are a classic garnish: perch a slice on the edge of the glass or use a vegetable peeler to make twists of citrus rind.

GRENADINE

A sweet red flavoring syrup made from pomegranate juice. It adds delicate sweetness and a pretty pink color to a drink.

HERBS

Fresh herb garnishes add pleasing aromatics, and those with long stems, like rosemary, lavender, and thyme, look especially elegant in highball and collins glasses.

ICE

Ice is a vital ingredient of every mocktail—very rarely should a mocktail be warm. You should have a generous supply of ice cubes as well as crushed ice. If no ice crusher is available, place a cup of ice cubes in a tea towel and bash it against the wall to shatter the ice. You can also place it on a hard surface in a tea towel and smack it with a hammer or rolling pin.

Add an exciting finishing touch to any drink with flavored ice. Freeze an ice tray of undiluted lemon juice, lime juice, or other fruit juice as an attractive and flavorful addition to a drink. You can also create mint ice cubes by placing a mint leaf in each section of the ice tray, filling it with water, and then freezing it.

Adding juices, fruits, or herbs to your ice cube tray before freezing is an unexpected way to add visual appeal and subtle flavor to your drinks.

Coffee Ice Cubes

As the ice cubes in a beverage melt, the beverage is diluted. For cold mixed drinks prepared with coffee, using coffee ice cubes will help maintain the flavor. Note that coffee is strong and will taint the plastic of an ice cube tray, so you'll want to have a tray solely for use with coffee. Trays may be filled with brewed coffee or espresso shots—one per square. You can also freeze coffee and cream for a light brown cube that will add flavor and a visually interesting marbled pattern to your drink. You should use pleasant coffee blends that aren't roasted too dark since very strong coffee flavor profiles could compete with your drink flavors.

ORGEAT

A sweet syrup with a distinctive almond flavor. Used for adding sweetness and nuttiness.

SHRUBS

A concoction of equal parts sugar, fruit, and vinegar that can be mixed with spirits, sparkling wine, beer, and sparkling water. Shrubs can be made with any kind of fruit, sweetener, or vinegar; apple cider vinegar and wine or champagne vinegars are the best choices to add a hint of acidity and sourness. Enjoy experimenting with different combinations.

Shrub Preparation Methods

Many of the recipes in this book can be personalized or adjusted by using custom syrups or shrubs. Create your own unique mixers using one of the following techniques. *All recipes make roughly 1 cup (240ml) of shrub; multiply the quantities to scale up the production if you like the recipe or have a lot of fruit to use up before it goes bad.*

Basic Shrub

Chop up 1 cup (100–200g) fruit. Stir fruit and 1 cup (200g) sugar together until incorporated, then stir in 1 cup (240ml) vinegar. Cover and let sit for twenty-four to forty-eight hours in the refrigerator. Strain the liquid and discard the solids.

Hot-Process Shrub

Chop up 2 cups (200–400g) fruit. Stir fruit and 1 cup (200g) sugar together until incorporated, then stir in 1 cup (240ml) vinegar. Bring the mixture to a boil, then reduce to a simmer and let cook on low or medium-low heat for ten to fifteen minutes or until the fruit starts falling apart. Let cool completely, strain the liquid, and discard the solids.

Two-Stage Shrub

This method requires a little more time, but allows you to eat the fruit afterward. Chop up 1 cup (100–200g) fruit. Stir fruit and 1 cup (200g) sugar together until incorporated. Cover and let sit for twenty-four to forty-eight hours in the refrigerator. Strain the liquid and set aside the sugary solids to snack on or use in desserts. Mix the strained liquid with 1 cup (240ml) vinegar, cover, and let sit for another twenty-four hours in the refrigerator.

SIMPLE SYRUP

The easiest way to add sweetness to a drink is to use prepared simple syrup, also known as sugar syrup. It's easy to make. Heat two parts of sugar and one part of water in a saucepan and stir until the sugar has dissolved. Allow to cool and store in a suitable bottle, ready for use. It can be kept for at least a week before the sugar starts to crystallize. To sweeten basic simple syrup, add additional sugar or switch in brown sugar, turbinado sugar, honey, or maple syrup. Other flavors can be added to simple syrups to mix things up. See Not-So-Simple Syrup Recipes, page 29.

SOUR MIX

Sour mix adds a clean, sour tang to any drink. Make it in advance and keep it in the fridge. Squeeze about six large lemons or limes into a jar or cocktail shaker and add an equal quantity of water, two tablespoons (25g) of caster sugar, and the white of one egg (the egg white is optional, but will provide the foaminess of using traditional sour mix). Shake well and set aside until needed. (Any liquid containing egg should not be stored for more than a couple of days and should not be ingested by pregnant women and the elderly.) Alternatively, you can mix equal parts of lemon or lime juice and simple syrup, shaking vigorously with ice.

SYRUPS, VARIOUS FLAVORS

Along with the cocktail syrups mentioned on page 15, it can be helpful to have sweeter syrups available for use in dessert drinks. You can find a whole range of these flavored syrups in your local supermarket, often marketed as ice cream toppings or coffee flavorings. It helps to add variety to have a few of these in your bar supplies. Chocolate syrup is useful, as are the various fruit- and berry-flavored syrups.

Stocking your bar with a variety of syrups, from dessert-like chocolate and fruit syrups to coffee mixer favorites like caramel, vanilla, and hazelnut, can provide a lot of flavor flexibility to your drinks.

TABASCO SAUCE

This hot sauce is made with three ingredients: red pepper, high-grain vinegar, and a small amount of salt. Use it sparingly to add a kick to savory drinks.

WORCESTERSHIRE SAUCE

This dark brown condiment is widely used in both dishes and drinks. Vinegar, chili peppers, soy sauce, and anchovies are among its many ingredients. It is a main ingredient of the Bloody Mary and the alcohol-free version, the Virgin Mary.

Not-So-Simple Syrup Recipes

Switching out the sugar for honey or flavoring the syrup with herbs, fruits, or vegetables can make some magical drink mixers. *All recipes make roughly 2 cups (480ml) of simple syrup.*

Mint Simple Syrup

Heat 2 cups (400g) sugar and 2 cups (480ml) water over high heat, stirring constantly until the sugar is completely dissolved. Remove from heat, add 1 cup (30g) mint leaves, stir, and cover; let sit at room temperature for two hours. Strain mint leaves before use. You can also replace mint with basil, lemon verbena, chamomile, sage, or any other herbs growing in your garden.

Lavender Simple Syrup

Heat 2 cups (400g) sugar and 2 cups (480ml) water over high heat, stirring constantly until sugar is completely dissolved. Stir in either 1 cup (128g) fresh lavender blossoms or ½ cup (64g) dried lavender blossoms, remove from heat, cover, and let sit at room temperature for two hours. Strain the blossoms away before use. Use the same recipe with juniper berries instead of lavender to create a simple syrup that will add a gin-like flavor to your mocktails.

Rhubarb Simple Syrup

Heat 2 cups (400g) sugar and 2 cups (480ml) water over high heat, stirring constantly until sugar is completely dissolved. Add 4 pounds (1.8kg) of rhubarb chunks, reduce the heat to medium, and let simmer for about five minutes. Remove from heat and let cool. Once cooled, strain the liquid and discard the solids.

Hibiscus Simple Syrup

In a medium-sized pot, bring 2 cups (400g) sugar, 2 cups (480ml) water, and either 4 cups (180g) fresh hibiscus flowers or 2 cups (80g) dried hibiscus flowers to a boil over medium-high heat. Turn off the heat and allow to cool and steep at room temperature for two or more hours. Strain, then chill.

Mixing Alcohol-Free Cocktails

CONTRIBUTED BY LAURA WILLOUGHBY MBE, FOUNDER OF CLUB SODA, A COMMUNITY OF MINDFUL DRINKERS WITH MEMBERS ALL OVER THE WORLD. VISIT *JOINCLUBSODA.COM* AND FOLLOW *@JOINCLUBSODA* ON SOCIAL MEDIA.

Now that you've stocked your bar with alcohol-free beers, wines, and spirits, you're ready to mix, match, and explore. Use unique botanicals to create zingy gin-like moments, spicy and warming spirits for cozy evenings in, or your favorite zero-proof liquor with mood-enhancing ingredients to transform cocktail hour.

Whether you are doing a dry January or just cutting down on drinking, mixing your own alcohol-free cocktails is a perfect solution. It's an approach to changing your drinking habits that's worked well for many people. So how can you mix a perfect non-alcoholic cocktail at home?

Laura Willoughby MBE, founder of the global mindful drinking community Club Soda, wants to change the narrative around drinking and sobriety.

CHOOSE YOUR SPIRIT

The flavors some brands have created without needing alcohol to bump up the volume are amazing. Lyre's has a full range of spirits designed to replicate your favorites that can easily swap into any cocktail recipe. There are bitter aperitif-style drinks like those from Everleaf that can be served on the rocks or lengthened with soda or an alcohol-free sparkling wine. A stunning array of clear spirits replicate the feel of a gin and tonic, such as Mahala Botanical or drinks from Caleño. Spirits with spicy vanilla notes are great for giving a warm feeling on a chilly evening, and those with herbs and adaptogenic mushrooms, such as Three Spirit Nightcap, can possibly enhance your mood or have calming effects.

FIND THE PERFECT GLASS AND EXPERIMENT WITH MEASURES

The process of creating a drink is part of the treat. Finding and using an interesting glass is part of the experience of mixing unusual and enjoyable drinks at home. You can go large with an alcohol-free spirit and not worry about the headache tomorrow. Do what works for you or follow the creator's recommendations on the bottle.

PAY ATTENTION TO ICE

Oftentimes, for drinks mixed with alcohol-free spirits, the bigger the ice, the better. Small cubes will dilute the drink, whereas a big cube or sphere will chill it and keep it cold until you have finished. Invest in a giant ice cube tray. Shaken or poured over ice, your spirit will thank you for it.

SELECT YOUR MIXER

Alcohol-free spirits are designed to go with a mixer. They really do come alive when perfectly combined. A strong, overpoweringly bitter tonic can overwhelm more delicate flavors, so be fussy when it comes to mixers. Experiment with soda water as well as traditional tonics. Ginger ales also go well with dark spirits. Double Dutch has a fantastic selection of good quality mixers that complement alcohol-free spirits. If you are using cola, go for something lower sugar and good quality, like Karma Cola or Square Root sodas.

FINISH WITH A GARNISH

A good garnish brings an additional layer of aroma to a drink. Clap mint between your hands to release the smell and place sprigs of rosemary and thyme into your glass. Along with herbs, fruits and vegetables used as garnishes will add an entirely new dimension to an alcohol-free drink.

STORE YOUR SPIRIT CAREFULLY

Alcohol is a preservative, so that bottle of holiday ouzo at the back of the cupboard can last forever. Not so with alcohol-free spirits. Remember to always keep them in the fridge once opened and enjoy them often!

Shaken or Stirred?

Each recipe includes instructions on how to treat the ingredients to bring out the best in them. Some drink recipes call for the ingredients to be shaken or stirred. And sometimes a recipe will tell you the drink should be "built" or layered. So, why the difference?

It's all a matter of getting the ingredients combined correctly. Vigorously shaking a drink in an ice-filled cocktail shaker will thoroughly combine, slightly dilute, and chill the drink. For drinks that contain a fizzy ingredient like soda water or ginger ale, you should shake the rest of the ingredients first, then add the fizzy ingredient and stir gently. When you want the drinker to experience a series of consecutive flavors rather than one flavor throughout, you should build the drink, adding one ingredient carefully on top of the previous one.

Glossary

Every human activity, from hang-gliding to hunting has its own vocabulary. You don't necessarily have to know every word in the book, but it does help to be able to toss in the occasional correct word or phrase, just to show you know what you're doing.

The same, of course, applies to cocktail mixing—whether alcoholic or not. You can always say something like "throw in some of that yellow stuff," but it sounds a lot more professional to say "float a little Galliano on the surface." The following list of cocktail terms might come in handy, especially if you want to impress your sophisticated friends with your familiarity with cocktail talk.

Apéritif—A drink served before a meal, usually with a dryish flavor, to stimulate the appetite.

Blending—Ingredients with different textures, like fruit, ice, and juice, can be mixed to a smooth consistency by placing them in an electric blender and running it for a few seconds. An effective way of achieving a homogenous mixture.

Build—To "build" a drink, one ingredient is poured directly on top of the previous one in the glass, and not stirred, so the drinker encounters each layer of flavor one by one.

Cup—A measure sometimes referred to in this book. Not necessarily an exact quantity, although the official American cup contains 8 fluid ounces of liquid and the metric cup contains 250 ml. For the purposes of cocktail mixing, you can generally use an ordinary teacup. Size is often immaterial.

Dash—A dash is a small splash, usually used to denote the quantity of strongly flavored ingredients, like bitters or lime juice.

Digestif—A drink served at the end of a meal to settle the digestion. Usually fairly sweet, like a port or liqueur.

Flip—A flip is a drink made with an egg as a main ingredient. Usually smooth and creamy in texture and rich in flavor.

Float—Either a drink made by adding a scoop of ice cream on the top of a glass of carbonated drink (usually a cola) or the method of adding an ingredient very carefully on the previous layer of a cocktail so the colors are perfectly separated. The best way to float one ingredient on to another is to pour it slowly over the back of a spoon into the glass.

Garnish—Any solid ingredient used to decorate a cocktail. This could be a cherry on a cocktail stick, or a slice of fruit placed over the rim of the glass. Other common garnishes include cocktail olives, strawberries, celery stalks (for drinks like the Virgin Mary), fresh mint sprigs, and twists of citrus peel (see Twist, below). A garnish should ideally be simple and edible. Small paper umbrellas can feel a bit dated.

Ice—An essential ingredient for cocktails. Purists insist that ice should never be used more than once, and the most fussy bartenders claim that ice made in a domestic fridge freezes too slowly and is too "wet" for cocktail use. They prefer professionally made flash-frozen ice, which lasts longer and melts slowly.

Jigger—A small measure used by professional bartenders to obtain the correct amount of liquid. Similar to the "pony" (see Pony, below), containing roughly three tablespoons (44ml) of liquid.

Muddle—Some ingredients, particularly combinations of dry and wet (like mint or herbs and soda water) are "muddled together" by crushing them with the back of a spoon or special muddler.

Neat—A drink is served "neat" when it has no ice or mixer added to it.

Pony—An American cocktail measure containing 1 fl. oz. (30ml) of liquid, or roughly two tablespoons.

Punch—A large party drink, usually made in a bowl or basin, in quantities large enough to serve a whole party.

Rimmed—The rim of a glass can be "rimmed" with sugar or salt by moistening it with lemon juice or one of the ingredients of the drink, then pressing it into a saucer of caster sugar or salt so that the grains stick to the damp glass rim. The effect is very attractive and adds flavor and texture to the drink.

Rocks (on the)—when a drink is described as "on the rocks," it has been poured over ice cubes in the glass in which it is served.

Scoop—An ice scoop is a handy utensil for transferring ice cubes or crushed ice from the ice bucket to the glass. No specific sizes needed, but usually containing about half a cup.

Shaken—This refers to a drink that is mixed by placing it in a cocktail shaker with ice cubes, and then shaken vigorously before being strained into a cocktail glass.

Stirred—This is the method used to mix ingredients when not too much brisk shaking is required. Usually used when one of the ingredients is carbonated (for example, soda water) to retain the bubbles.

Twist—A twist is a longish strip of peel (usually lemon or orange) twisted into a pretty shape and dropped into a drink. This has two results: it adds flavor and aroma and enhances the appearance of a drink.

Zest—The oily aromatic substance that is found in the outer layer of citrus peels. Twisting a little lemon peel over a drink will spray it with the fresh zest aroma.

CHAPTER 1:
New Signature Mocktails

Alcohol-free drinking is having a bit of a renaissance and many companies and professional mixologists have been making huge strides toward creating zero-proof spirits, botanicals, mixes, and mocktails to suit every kind of drink enthusiast. There are alcohol-free wines, near beers, and liqueur substitutes that can be used to add unique flavors to your own drinks, and bottled booze-free cocktails that bring the subtle tastes and unusual combinations of their alcoholic cousins straight to your fridge. The following chapter features exceptional signature drinks from a few of these trailblazing innovators.

Try
this rich
Blackberry
"Bold" Fashioned.
Recipe on
page 52.

Raspberry Smash

This light refreshing drink starts with one of Amethyst's distinctive non-alcoholic botanical spirits and adds muddled fresh raspberries for a bright, sweet twist.

INGREDIENTS

- 3 fl. oz. (90ml) Amethyst Blueberry Ginger Mint
- 1½ fl. oz. (45ml) soda water
- ¼ fl. oz. (7ml) simple syrup
- ½ fl. oz. (15ml) raspberry citrus shrub, Amethyst used Rhoot Man Beverage Company's
- 3 muddled raspberries
- Ice
- Raspberries and mint sprig, for garnish

METHOD

1. Muddle the raspberries into the bottom of your glass.
2. Add Amethyst, soda water, shrub, and simple syrup.
3. Stir, top with ice, and garnish with raspberries and mint.

AMETHYST SPIRITS
JANE HARMON

Burnt Church Distillery Owners Billy and Sean Watterson crafted Amethyst distilled botanical spirits for the 20% of bar, distillery, and brewery patrons that choose not to drink alcohol. The word amethyst comes from the Greek word *amethustos*, which means "not drunk." Brand ambassador Jane Harmon grew up on Hilton Head Island and loves the small-town feel of Bluffton and the Lowcountry. She has been in food and beverage almost her entire life as a server, bartender, event planner, and manager.

Mulled Ginger Cider

Chef Paul Eschbach loves ginger and turmeric tea. He also loves a warm cup of mulled cider in the winter. It turns out that the two go together perfectly. The classic pairing of apple and ginger combined with the earthiness of turmeric is perfect with the darker notes of cider. This drink includes mulling spices for more wintery flavors but have fun and use whatever you like.

INGREDIENTS

- 6 fl. oz. (180ml) Betera Ginger-Orange
- 3 fl. oz. (90ml) apple or pear cider
- 1 clove, 1 cinnamon stick or star anise OR 1 Tbsp. (8.5g) mulling spices
- 2 Tbsp. (30ml) maple syrup
- Candied ginger, for garnish

METHOD

1. Heat all ingredients together and stir until desired temperature and spice flavor is reached.
2. Garnish with candied ginger on a skewer or on the side.

BETERA
CHEF PAUL ESCHBACH

Betera founders Nick Benz, Paul Eschbach, and Aaron Sanchez are three guys who've had a few drinks, but they started thinking about ways to be healthier when they began growing their families. They started Betera to create complex, unique, and low-in-sugar drinks that could replace alcohol.

Blackberry Whiskey Sour

This is a classic non-alcoholic cocktail inspired by drinks from the Prohibition era. It mixes Blind Tiger's Bee's Knees and fresh blackberries, then adds a kick with your favorite alcohol-free whiskey. Drinks with raw egg are best avoided by pregnant women and the elderly.

RECIPE BY ELIZABETH HEFFERNAN

INGREDIENTS

- 1½ fl. oz. (45ml) alcohol-free whiskey, Elizabeth used Spiritless Kentucky 74
- 2 fl. oz. (60ml) Blind Tiger Bee's Knees
- 3 blackberries
- 1 egg white
- Ice
- Blackberries or a lemon wheel, for garnish

METHOD

1. Muddle blackberries in a cocktail shaker.
2. Add whiskey, Bee's Knees, and egg white to the shaker.
3. Dry shake (no ice), then add ice and hard shake for 30 to 45 seconds.
4. Double strain into a coupe glass or rocks glass. Garnish with blackberries or a lemon wheel.

BLIND TIGER SPIRIT-FREE COCKTAILS
REBECCA STYN, PH.D.

Rebecca Styn, Ph.D., is the founder and managing partner of Blind Tiger Spirit-Free Cocktails, a line of non-alcoholic cocktails and mixers inspired by the classic drinks from the Prohibition era. She also serves as proprietor of Room 33 Speakeasy in Erie, PA, USA. Led by mixologist Elizabeth Heffernan, Room 33 Speakeasy created take-home versions of their favorite cocktails to mirror the flavors of the originals without including the alcohol. The name "Blind Tiger" came from a common nickname for speakeasies used during Prohibition.

Monday Whiskey Mule

This mule alternative packs the same ginger kick as other alcoholic versions. Blended with lime and alcohol-free whiskey, it's a delicious refreshing zinger to add to a night out.

INGREDIENTS

- 2 fl. oz. (60ml) Monday Zero Alcohol Whiskey
- ½ fl. oz. (15ml) fresh lime juice
- Ice
- Ginger beer
- Fresh mint, for garnish

METHOD

1. Add whiskey and lime juice to a cocktail shaker with ice.
2. Shake until cold and strain over fresh ice in your favorite short glass or copper mug.
3. Top with ginger beer and garnish with fresh mint.

DRINK MONDAY INC.
CHRIS BOYD

Drink Monday is a company focused on helping people prioritize self-care and wellness and promoting good health and great taste. Co-founder and CEO Chris Boyd takes great pleasure in listening to people open up about their challenges with alcohol and their pivot toward a life with less of that stuff in it. He is honored to have something he loves play a role in helping people stay the course and achieve their goals.

Spiritless Bombay Fire Drill

This drink blends sweet, smoky flavors and light grapefruit juice. The final touch is homemade pomegranate agave syrup to build upon the sweet burn of the Bombay Fire.

INGREDIENTS

- 2 fl. oz. (60ml) alcohol-free whiskey, Michael used Spiritless Kentucky 74
- ¾ fl. oz. (22ml) grapefruit juice
- ½ fl. oz. (15ml) pomegranate agave syrup*
- 4 fl. oz. (120ml) Mocktail Club Bombay Fire
- Ice
- Pomegranate seeds and 1 toasted cinnamon stick, for garnish

*Pomegranate agave syrup

Combine equal parts pomegranate seeds and agave in a pot and bring to a boil, stirring occasionally. Let simmer for 10 minutes on low heat to reduce.

METHOD

1. Combine whiskey, grapefruit juice, and pomegranate agave syrup in a cocktail shaker and shake for 5 to 7 seconds.
2. Add Bombay Fire to the shaker and pour over ice in a double rocks glass.
3. Garnish with a sprinkle of pomegranate seeds and toasted cinnamon stick.

M O C K T A I L
C L U B®

MOCKTAIL CLUB

Mocktail Club is a line of ready-to-drink non-alcoholic cocktails that recreate the complexity of cocktails without the alcohol. They use ingredients like superfruits and prebiotics to create drinks that redefine the social drinking experience and allow everyone to celebrate together.

RECIPE BY MICHAEL TOSCANO,
NATIONAL DIRECTOR OF TRADE
MARKETING, SPIRITLESS

Non-Alcoholic Margarita

This recipe is an alcohol-free version of the iconic Tommy's Margarita from San Francisco. You can use any non-alcoholic tequila you prefer, but The Dry Goods Beverage Company particularly likes it with Ritual Zero Proof Tequila Alternative for a fresh, spicy drink or with Free Spirits The Spirit of Tequila for a more mellow rendition.

INGREDIENTS

- 2 fl. oz. (60ml) alcohol-free tequila
- 1 fl. oz. (30ml) fresh lime juice
- ½ fl. oz. (15ml) agave syrup
- Ice
- Lime wheel, for garnish

METHOD

1. Combine all ingredients in a cocktail shaker or mason jar with ice and shake briefly to chill.
2. Strain into a rocks glass over fresh ice or without ice in a margarita glass and garnish with a lime wheel.

THE DRY GOODS BEVERAGE COMPANY
ADRIENNE STILLMAN KRAUSZ

Adrienne Stillman Krausz is the co-founder of The Dry Goods Beverage Company, an online store for non-alcoholic wine, spirits, and cocktail alternatives (*www.drygoodsdrinks.com*). After writing two books about (alcoholic) cocktails and working in wine for 10 years, she and her husband Jake Krausz started Dry Goods to showcase the incredible new alcohol-free products becoming available. They both strongly believe that everyone deserves a great drink—whether it has alcohol in it or not.

Aretha Franklin

Create the lightly frothed effect for this gorgeous drink using a handheld frother, a useful tool for bartenders and baristas alike.

INGREDIENTS

- ¼ tsp. (1.25ml) honey
- Cacao powder
- 2 fl. oz. (60ml) dragonfruit juice
- ⅛ tsp. (0.6ml) vanilla extract
- 3 fl. oz. (90ml) Ferm Fatale iKonic Water

METHOD

1. Dab honey on one edge of a martini glass and roll the rim on a plate with cacao to collect.
2. In a mixing vessel, froth the dragonfruit juice with the vanilla extract.
3. Pour the frothed mixture into the martini glass.
4. Top up with iKonic Water and serve.

**FERM FATALE
JULIE CIELO**

Ferm Fatale is a line of zero-sugar, wildly fermented, organic, ready-to-drink mocktails intended to provide a healthier choice for social drinking. Ferm Fatale's beverages are local, seasonal, small-batch drinks that are high in B vitamins, good bacteria, yeast, and enzymes. Ferm Fatale founder Julie Cielo is a medium, mortician, yoga therapist, and transformational life coach who grew up fermenting with her Italian-immigrant grandfather in rural Pennsylvania.

Noughty Peppermint Spritzer

The mint and lemon in this spritzer combine to create a light, refreshing drink that will sparkle at any event with any meal.

INGREDIENTS

- 2½ fl. oz. (75ml) prepared peppermint tea, cooled
- 2 tsp. (10ml) fresh lemon juice
- 1 tsp. (5ml) simple syrup
- Ice
- Noughty Alcohol-Free Organic Sparkling Wine
- Lemon wheel and mint sprig, for garnish

METHOD

1. Add tea, lemon juice, simple syrup, and ice to a cocktail shaker and shake.
2. Strain over ice in a wine glass.
3. Top up with sparkling wine and garnish with the lemon wheel and mint sprig.

THOMSON & SCOTT
NOUGHTY
AMANDA THOMSON

British entrepreneur and Thomson & Scott founder and CEO Amanda Thomson launched Noughty Organic Sparkling Chardonnay in 2019 as the first alcohol-free, organic, vegan sparkling chardonnay on the market. Noughty's drinks have almost half the sugar content of traditional alcohol-free sparkling wines and are halal certified, making them a good choice for those seeking delicious alcohol-free wines that stand up against their alcoholic counterparts.

Absentini

This drink starts with Isn't Distinctivo Absence. Absence is many things: herbaceous, lightly bitter, and citrusy, to name a few, but it isn't "hot" until you create the Absentini. Add sliced jalapeños or serrano peppers depending on your preference and rim the glass with Tajín Clásico Seasoning for a kick of salty lime. Absence makes the heat grow fonder!

INGREDIENTS

- 1 bottle Isn't Distinctivo Absence
- 1 to 2 slices jalapeño or serrano pepper, to taste
- Lime juice
- Tajín Clásico Seasoning
- 1 cucumber slice, to float
- 1 cucumber slice and 1 jalapeño or serrano pepper slice, for garnish

METHOD

1. Rub the rim of a martini glass with lime juice and coat with Tajín Clásico Seasoning.
2. In a mixing vessel, gently stir the Absence with the pepper slices, then pour into the martini glass.
3. Float the cucumber slice on top, then garnish with an additional cucumber slice and pepper slice.

ISN'T DRINKS
NICK GRUBE AND JACKIE VERILLI

Nick and Jackie of Isn't Drinks often spent social evenings trying Nick's home brews, but when Jackie began trying to limit the number of alcoholic drinks she had at social gatherings, she realized she was sick of the usual alternatives (soda pops, club soda with lime, iced tea). Nick agreed and they have been co-creating Isn't Drinks ever since!

Chile Pomegranate Paloma

A spicy twist on this bubbly tequila classic, it's loaded with amino acids and vitamins B3 and B6, making this cocktail a delicious and lively immune booster.

The Free Spirits Company craft non-alcoholic spirit alternatives including bourbon, gin, and tequila through a process called distillate reconstruction. These alternatives distill the natural essences of American White Oak, European Juniper, and Mexican Blue Agave, and infuses them with vitamins B3 and B6 and amino acids like taurine for that little something extra. Steve Turner, founder of consulting company The Brit Behind Bars, was motivated to collaborate with Free Spirits based on how well their products work in the creation of intriguing vibrant cocktails without alcohol.

THE FREE SPIRITS COMPANY
STEVE TURNER

INGREDIENTS

- 3 fl. oz. (90ml) Free Spirits The Spirit of Tequila
- ¾ fl. oz. (22ml) spiced pomegranate grenadine*
- 1 fl. oz. (30ml) pink grapefruit juice
- Sparkling water, Steve used Topo Chico

*Spiced pomegranate grenadine

In a saucepan add 1 cup (200g) of sugar, 1 cup (240ml) of 100% pomegranate juice, the entire peel of an orange, and 6 broken dried chiles de árbol. Bring to a boil and simmer for 15 minutes. Let cool, strain into a jar, and store in the refrigerator for up to 2 weeks.

METHOD

1. Add all the ingredients to an iced cocktail shaker.
2. Shake and strain into a tall glass and top with sparkling water.
3. Garnish with a grapefruit slice and a dried árbol chile.

VeryVery Berry Bellini

This refreshing berry-filled beverage starts with Mingle's Blackberry Hibiscus Bellini, and contrasts its delicate sweetness against the bitters and the grenadine.

INGREDIENTS

- 4 fl. oz. (120ml) Mingle Blackberry Hibiscus Bellini
- 2 to 3 dashes aromatic bitters
- 2 dashes grenadine
- 1 splash soda water
- Ice
- Fresh berries, for garnish

METHOD

1. Pour Bellini, bitters, and grenadine in a cocktail shaker and blend with a stirring spoon.
2. Pour over ice in a rocks glass.
3. Top with a splash of soda water and garnish with fresh berries.

**MINGLE MOCKTAILS
LAURA TAYLOR**

Years ago, Laura Taylor, Mingle Mocktails founder and booze-free badass, made the decision to give up alcohol and found it to be a lot more difficult than she anticipated. At social events, she often felt out of place and not part of the group, so she created Mingle for anyone giving up drinking for the night, week, or as a lifestyle change to still feel included and be a part of the party.

Ward 8 Cocktail

The story goes that the drink that inspired Blind Tiger's smoky citrus Ward 8 mix was created to honor Boston's Ward 8, a district that historically delivered a winning margin in the election of a powerful democratic boss in 1898.

INGREDIENTS

- 4 fl. oz. (120ml) Blind Tiger Ward 8
- 2 fl. oz. (60ml) alcohol-free whiskey
- Ice
- Orange peel, for garnish

METHOD

1. Pour ingredients into a cocktail shake and shake.
2. Pour into your favorite martini or coupe glass and garnish with an orange peel.

BLIND TIGER SPIRIT-FREE COCKTAILS
REBECCA STYN, PH.D.

Rebecca Styn, Ph.D., is the founder and managing partner of Blind Tiger Spirit-Free Cocktails, a line of non-alcoholic cocktails and mixers inspired by the classic drinks from the Prohibition era. She also serves as proprietor of Room 33 Speakeasy in Erie, PA, USA. Led by mixologist Elizabeth Heffernan, Room 33 Speakeasy created take-home versions of their favorite cocktails to mirror the flavors of the originals without including the alcohol. The name "Blind Tiger" came from a common nickname for speakeasies used during Prohibition.

The Garden Variety

Start your day with this refreshing and nuanced cocktail with everything green from your garden.

The Free Spirits Company craft non-alcoholic spirit alternatives including bourbon, gin, and tequila through a process called distillate reconstruction. These alternatives distill the natural essences of American White Oak, European Juniper, and Mexican Blue Agave, and infuses them with vitamins B3 and B6 and amino acids like taurine for that little something extra. Steve Turner, founder of consulting company The Brit Behind Bars, was motivated to collaborate with Free Spirits based on how well their products work in the creation of intriguing vibrant cocktails without alcohol.

**THE FREE SPIRITS COMPANY
STEVE TURNER**

INGREDIENTS

- 2½ fl. oz. (75ml) Free Spirits The Spirit of Gin
- 1½ fl. oz. (45ml) garden mix*
- ½ fl. oz. (15ml) lime juice
- 2 dashes cucumber bitters
- 2 dashes celery bitters
- 2 dashes saline
- Ice
- Celery leaf, mint, and a pinch of black pepper, for garnish

*Garden mix

Add 1 cup (100g) chopped celery, 1 cup (149g) chopped green bell pepper, a handful of parsley, 1 cup (98g) trimmed snap peas, 2 cups (480ml) agave, and 1 cup (240ml) water to a blender. Blend until smooth and strain out the solids.

METHOD

1. Add all the ingredients to a cocktail shaker and shake.
2. Strain into a coupe glass and garnish with the celery leaf, mint, and a pinch of black pepper.

Mocktail Club's Blackberry "Bold" Fashioned

This drink uses some of the traditional ingredients and techniques used to create the popular Old Fashioned cocktail, but adds a sweet berry twist.

INGREDIENTS

- 5 fl. oz. (150ml) Mocktail Club Manhattan Berry
- 5 blackberries, plus more for garnish
- 3 dashes aromatic bitters
- Ice
- 1 large sprig rosemary, for garnish

METHOD

1. Combine all the ingredients in a cocktail shaker and muddle for 10 to 15 seconds.
2. Add a generous handful of ice and shake for 10 to 15 seconds or until the shaker becomes frosted.
3. Strain through a sieve into a rocks glass over a large ice cube and garnish with blackberries and fresh rosemary.

MOCKTAIL CLUB

Mocktail Club is a line of ready-to-drink non-alcoholic cocktails that recreate the complexity of cocktails without the alcohol. They use ingredients like superfruits and prebiotics to create drinks that redefine the social drinking experience and allow everyone to celebrate together.

Pom Basil Shrub

This is a refreshing sangria alternative that blends sweet and tart pomegranate flavor with basil and balsamic vinegar.

INGREDIENTS

- 1 bottle Mocktails Sansgria
- 3 Tbsp. fresh pomegranate seeds
- 6 fresh basil leaves
- 1 tsp. balsamic vinegar
- Ice
- 1 bunch basil, for garnish

METHOD

1. Add the pomegranate seeds, basil leaves, balsamic vinegar, and a splash of Sansgria to a cocktail shaker and muddle well.
2. Fill ⅓ of the cocktail shaker with ice and shake vigorously for 5 to 8 seconds.
3. Pour into a large wine glass or goblet and garnish with basil.

MOCKTAIL BEVERAGES, INC.
BILL GAMELLI

Mocktail Beverages was founded in 2018 by former Wall Street Executive Bill Gamelli and his two co-founding partners, Mark Guthrie and Jim Dowla, to create healthy, sophisticated beverages for every guest at the party. They worked with global award-winning mixologist Ezra Star to create their first four flavors and continue to source and combine natural, sustainable, and ethically sourced botanicals to create complex, delicious drinks.

Daisy Bell

This is a refreshing drink that blends the light dry finish of the SipClean White Blend with the subtle bitter orange spice of the bitter aperitif syrup.

INGREDIENTS

- ½ can SipClean White Blend
- 1 fl. oz. (30ml) bitter aperitif syrup, Shannon used Giffard Aperitif Syrup
- 2 fl. oz. (60ml) mineral water
- Ice
- 1 large orange slice, for garnish

METHOD

1. Combine all the ingredients in a rocks glass, then add the ice.
2. Garnish with a large orange slice.

SIPC
ALEXANDRIA KLEMPF
AND SHANNON MICHELLE

SipC was founded by Alexandria Klempf in 2019 with a focus on creating alcohol-removed wines for women at any stage of their lives. SipC aims to help women feel good about consuming adult beverages: drinks with less calories, less sugar, and zero hangovers. Shannon Michelle is the lead bartender at Sidecar in Jacksonville, FL, USA. With over 12 years in the service industry, she spearheads one of the premier beverage programs in Northeast Florida, is regularly active in the competition circuit, and freelances as a cocktail consultant for restaurants, brands, and events.

Booze-Free Penicillin

The Penicillin is one of Douglas's very favorite cocktails, especially in the wintertime. For him, the fresh lemon juice, smoky and peaty Islay malt Scotch whiskey, and the bit of sweetness and bite from the ginger liqueur is just about perfect. When Douglas began monitoring and reducing his alcohol consumption, he wanted to make an alcohol-free version that would pay homage to the traditional Penicillin. The decadent, woody smoothness and hint of black pepper spice of Three Spirit Nightcap holds up well as an alternative for the Scotch.

SPIRITED AWAY

SPIRITED AWAY NEW YORK

Douglas Watters founded Spirited Away in 2020 as New York's first booze-free bottle shop, dedicated to non-alcoholic spirits, wines, beers, cocktails, and more. In terms of results versus effort, Douglas has found that reducing or eliminating alcohol is one of the highest return-on-investment actions a person can take to improve their health, wellbeing, and happiness. It's a legitimate life hack.

SPIRITED AWAY NEW YORK
DOUGLAS WATTERS

INGREDIENTS

- 2 fl. oz. (60ml) Three Spirit Nightcap
- 1 fl. oz. (30ml) fresh squeezed lemon juice
- ¾ fl. oz. (22ml) ginger syrup
- Ice
- Candied ginger and lemon peel, for garnish

METHOD

1. Combine all ingredients in an ice-filled cocktail shaker or mason jar.
2. Shake hard and strain into an ice-filled whiskey tumbler.
3. Garnish with candied ginger and lemon peel.

Maze Runner

Isn't Drinks turned to coffee to fuel this dessert-like treasure. A rim of cinnamon brings out baking spice flavor, which pairs with the dark fruit to run circles around any traditional barista fare.

INGREDIENTS

- 1 bottle Isn't Distinctivo Mazy
- 2 fl. oz. (60ml) espresso, cooled to room temperature
- Half-and-half or cream, to taste
- Ice
- Ground cinnamon, for glass rim
- 1 star anise pod, to float

METHOD

1. Rim your preferred glass with ground cinnamon.
2. Combine the Mazy and espresso in a cocktail shaker and gently stir.
3. Place ice in the cinnamon-rimmed glass and pour the Mazy and espresso mixture over the ice.
4. Add half-and-half or cream to taste and float a star anise pod on top.

ISN'T DRINKS
NICK GRUBE AND JACKIE VERILLI

Nick and Jackie of Isn't Drinks often spent social evenings trying Nick's home brews, but when Jackie began trying to limit the number of alcoholic drinks she had at social gatherings, she realized she was sick of the usual alternatives (soda pops, club soda with lime, iced tea). Nick agreed and they have been co-creating Isn't Drinks ever since!

Noughty Classic

This simple drink adds unusual flavor to alcohol-free sparkling wine by infusing a sugar cube with bitters and adding in the aromatic essence of a lemon twist. The mint and lemon in this spritzer combine to create a light, refreshing drink that will sparkle at any event with any meal.

INGREDIENTS

- 1 white sugar cube
- 3 dashes aromatic bitters
- 4¼ fl. oz. (127ml) Noughty Alcohol-Free Organic Sparkling Wine
- Lemon twist, for garnish

METHOD

1. Sprinkle a few dashes of aromatic bitters over the sugar cube and drop the sugar cube into a chilled flute glass.
2. Fill the glass with the sparkling wine and garnish with the lemon twist.

THOMSON & SCOTT
NOUGHTY
AMANDA THOMSON

British entrepreneur and Thomson & Scott founder and CEO Amanda Thomson launched Noughty Organic Sparkling Chardonnay in 2019 as the first alcohol-free, organic, vegan sparkling chardonnay on the market. Noughty's drinks have almost half the sugar content of traditional alcohol-free sparkling wines and are halal certified, making them a good choice for those seeking delicious alcohol-free wines that stand up against their alcoholic counterparts.

Spiritless Whiskey Sour

This is a fresh, alcohol-free take on the classic whiskey sour. For a spicier kick, try replacing the simple syrup with a fiery ginger syrup. **Note:** If you include the egg whites, pregnant women and the elderly should avoid drinking.

INGREDIENTS

- 2 fl. oz. (60ml) Spiritless Kentucky 74
- 1 fl. oz. (30ml) fresh lemon juice
- ¾ fl. oz. (22ml) simple syrup
- ½ fl. oz. (15ml) egg whites, optional
- Ice
- 1 cherry and 1 orange wheel, for garnish

METHOD

1. Shake all the ingredients with ice in a cocktail shaker.
2. Strain into a highball or double rocks glass with fresh ice.
3. Garnish with the cherry and orange wheel.

**SPIRITLESS
DEREK BROWN**

Derek Brown is the owner of Washington, D.C.'s 2017 Spirited Award-winning "Best American Cocktail Bar," Columbia Room. He has also written a large number of books and articles on spirits, cocktails, and well-being. He's served as the chief spirits advisor to the National Archives and is a distinguished fellow at Catholic University's Ciocca Center for Principled Entrepreneurship. In 2020, Drinks International named him one of the Bar World 100, a list of the top beverage figures effecting positive change in the global bar industry. The same year, Brown joined Spiritless to serve as a brand champion and advisor. He is passionate about helping people learn how to use Spiritless products.

Mocktail Club's Havana Nights

The crushed juniper berries will add a light gin-like essence to the fresh and slightly spicy notes of Havana Twist.

INGREDIENTS

- 4 fl. oz. (120ml) Mocktail Club Havana Twist
- 1 Tbsp. (4.5g) juniper berries
- ½ tsp. (2.2g) brown sugar
- Ice
- 1 cucumber slice, for garnish

METHOD

1. Crush the juniper berries with the brown sugar and add them to the top of the strainer.
2. Pour the Havana Twist over the berry and sugar mixture on the strainer into a cocktail shaker filled with ice.
3. Shake well and strain into a cocktail glass.
4. Garnish with a slice of cucumber.

MOCKTAIL CLUB

Mocktail Club is a line of ready-to-drink non-alcoholic cocktails that recreate the complexity of cocktails without the alcohol. They use ingredients like superfruits and prebiotics to create drinks that redefine the social drinking experience and allow everyone to celebrate together.

Pineapple Espresso & Tonic

Mixing coffee and pineapple flavors might not seem obvious at first, but this unexpected drink is unique and interesting and will keep your friends and family on their toes.

Top Note Tonic founders Mary Pellettieri and Noah Swanson set out to start a company that could change the way people think about—and enjoy—drink mixers. They began to experiment with herbs and syrups in their self-constructed commercial kitchen and together they formulated a unique Bitter Orange Syrup, which they sold at local farmer's markets in Wisconsin. The response was so positive that they decided to bring their products to a broader audience and Top Note continues to add to the world of mixers with their innovative and high-quality products.

TOP NOTE TONIC
MARY PELLETTIERI

INGREDIENTS

- 2 fl. oz. (60ml) espresso
- 1 fl. oz. (30ml) pineapple syrup*
- 5 fl. oz. (150ml) Top Note Bitter Lemon Tonic Water
- Dehydrated pineapple, pineapple fronds, and fresh basil, for garnish

*Pineapple syrup

Combine 1 cup (240ml) of pineapple juice and 1 cup (200g) of sugar in a small pot over medium-high heat. Bring to a boil, then reduce heat and simmer for 5 minutes. Let cool before bottling. Store in the refrigerator and use within 2 weeks. Makes 8 fl. oz. (240ml) of syrup.

METHOD

1. Mix the espresso with the syrup and set aside.
2. Fill a glass with ice and add the Bitter Lemon Tonic Water.
3. Slowly pour the coffee and syrup mixture into the glass and garnish with the dehydrated pineapple, pineapple fronds, and fresh basil.

Maple Bourbon Old Fashioned

A muddle-free version of this festive classic that leaves your head less muddled too!

INGREDIENTS

- 3 fl. oz. (90ml) Free Spirits The Spirit of Bourbon
- ½ tsp. (2.5ml) bourbon barrel-aged maple syrup
- 1 dash aromatic bitters
- Ice
- 1 orange peel and cherry, for garnish

METHOD

1. Add all the ingredients to a cocktail shaker and half fill with ice.
2. Stir until chilled, then strain into a rocks glass with one large ice cube.
3. Express the oil of the orange peel over the drink by gently twisting the peel over the surface of the cocktail to add a thin float of essential oil and running the peel lightly over the rim of the glass.
4. Drop the twisted orange peel into the glass and drop in a cherry.

**THE FREE SPIRITS
COMPANY
STEVE TURNER**

The Free Spirits Company craft non-alcoholic spirit alternatives including bourbon, gin, and tequila through a process called distillate reconstruction. These alternatives distill the natural essences of American White Oak, European Juniper, and Mexican Blue Agave, and infuses them with vitamins B3 and B6 and amino acids like taurine for that little something extra. Steve Turner, founder of consulting company The Brit Behind Bars, was motivated to collaborate with Free Spirits based on how well their products work in the creation of intriguing vibrant cocktails without alcohol.

Rose Bush

This is the Isn't Drinks take on a shrub with the addition of apple cider vinegar. Their Redessence is floral, citrusy, and decidedly tart and the addition of apple cider vinegar shifts that tartness bravely towards sour. The lemon slice and rose petal float adds a unique look to the drink while adding a slight aromatic hint of flavor.

INGREDIENTS

- 1 bottle Isn't Distinctivo Redessence
- 2 tsp. (10ml) apple cider vinegar
- Lemon slice and rose petal or bud, for garnish

METHOD

1. Pour the Redessence into your preferred glass and gently stir in the apple cider vinegar.
2. Float the lemon slice and the rose petal or bud lightly on top.

ISN'T DRINKS
NICK GRUBE AND JACKIE VERILLI

Nick and Jackie of Isn't Drinks often spent social evenings trying Nick's home brews, but when Jackie began trying to limit the number of alcoholic drinks she had at social gatherings, she realized she was sick of the usual alternatives (soda pops, club soda with lime, iced tea). Nick agreed and they have been co-creating Isn't Drinks ever since!

The Noughty Singer

This light, delicious drink features the popular flavor combination of cherry and almond. It's a sweet, light drink that will add a bright touch to any event.

INGREDIENTS

- 1 maraschino cherry
- ½ tsp. (2ml) cherry juice
- 1 tsp. (5ml) orgeat syrup
- 4¼ fl. oz. (127ml) Noughty Alcohol-Free Organic Sparkling Wine

METHOD

1. Place the maraschino cherry and cherry juice into a chilled Nick & Nora glass.
2. Add the orgeat syrup.
3. Top up with the sparkling wine and gently stir.

RECIPE CREATED AT THE SINGER TAVERN, LONDON

**THOMSON & SCOTT
NOUGHTY
AMANDA THOMSON**

British entrepreneur and Thomson & Scott founder and CEO Amanda Thomson launched Noughty Organic Sparkling Chardonnay in 2019 as the first alcohol-free, organic, vegan sparkling chardonnay on the market. Noughty's drinks have almost half the sugar content of traditional alcohol-free sparkling wines and are halal certified, making them a good choice for those seeking delicious alcohol-free wines that stand up against their alcoholic counterparts.

Say *Ahhhhh*

This cucumber, watermelon, and mint zero-proof spritz is sure to give you *all* the spa vibes. Mix in as much of each ingredient as you'd like—this recipe is meant to be played with and made to suit your tastes. At first glance, it may sound complicated, but Laura encourages everyone to experiment in the kitchen, make mistakes, and have fun!

INGREDIENTS

- Fresh watermelon, cubed
- Fresh mint, to taste, plus more for garnish
- Ice cubes
- Coconut water
- 3 to 4 fl. oz. (90 to 120ml) DRY Cucumber Botanical Bubbly, chilled
- 1 to 2 fl. oz. (30 to 60ml) alcohol-free gin, Laura used Monday Zero Alcohol Gin
- 3 dashes ginger bitters, optional, Laura used Hella Cocktail Co. Ginger Cocktail Bitters

METHOD

1. Combine fresh watermelon, fresh mint, a couple of ice cubes, and small amount of coconut water in a blender.
2. Pour the blended mixture into ice cube trays and freeze it overnight.
3. Once frozen, pop a couple watermelon mint cubes into a glass of your choice and pour in the bubbly and gin.
4. If desired, pour a few dashes of ginger bitters into the glass, then top up with extra bubbly soda water and stir gently.
5. Garnish with fresh mint.

ZERO PROOF NATION
LAURA SILVERMAN

⚡ZEROPROOFNATION

Zero Proof Nation was born out of a desire to build authentic community around the zero-proof lifestyle, and to elevate the stories behind the beverages. Founder Laura Silverman's goal is to provide a platform highlighting non-alcoholic options to everyone who wants something different and new.

Bryan Boyce's Zarletti N/A Spritz

Milwaukee's Zarletti is serious about their non-alcoholic recipes, proving that this burgeoning category of drinks can be as innovative and complex as anything else on their menu. This spritz from Zarletti general manager Bryan Boyce mixes bold alcohol-free wine flavors with the bitter citrus of Top Note's Gentiana Tonic Water.

Top Note Tonic founders Mary Pellettieri and Noah Swanson set out to start a company that could change the way people think about—and enjoy—drink mixers. They began to experiment with herbs and syrups in their self-constructed commercial kitchen and together they formulated a unique Bitter Orange Syrup, which they sold at local farmer's markets in Wisconsin. The response was so positive that they decided to bring their products to a broader audience and Top Note continues to add to the world of mixers with their innovative and high-quality products.

TOP NOTE TONIC
MARY PELLETTIERI

INGREDIENTS

- 1 fl. oz. (30ml) alcohol-free red wine
- 3 fl. oz. (90ml) alcohol-free sparkling chardonnay, Bryan used Zera Chardonnay
- 3 fl. oz. (90ml) Top Note Gentiana Tonic Water
- 1 fresh orange wheel, for garnish
- Ice

METHOD

1. Fill a wine glass halfway with ice.
2. Add all the ingredients to the glass, stir gently, and garnish with an orange wheel.

RECIPE BY BRYAN BOYCE
GENERAL MANAGER
ZARLETTI, MILWAUKEE, WI, USA

Southside Cocktail

Supposedly the drink that inspired Blind Tiger's Southside was created in New York's 21 Club as part of its Prohibition-era menu (it was created several decades earlier at the Southside Sportsmen's Club in Long Island). It was reportedly mobster Al Capone's favorite drink.

INGREDIENTS

- 4 fl. oz. (120ml) Blind Tiger Southside
- 2 fl. oz. (60ml) alcohol-free gin
- Ice
- Orange peel, for garnish

METHOD

1. Pour the ingredients into a cocktail shaker over ice.
2. Shake and pour into your favorite martini or coupe glass; garnish with an orange peel.

BLIND TIGER SPIRIT-FREE COCKTAILS
REBECCA STYN, PH.D.

Rebecca Styn, Ph.D., is the founder and managing partner of Blind Tiger Spirit-Free Cocktails, a line of non-alcoholic cocktails and mixers inspired by the classic drinks from the Prohibition era. She also serves as proprietor of Room 33 Speakeasy in Erie, PA, USA. Led by mixologist Elizabeth Heffernan, Room 33 Speakeasy created take-home versions of their favorite cocktails to mirror the flavors of the originals without including the alcohol. The name "Blind Tiger" came from a common nickname for speakeasies used during Prohibition.

Fennel Raspberry Martini

This refreshing drink muddles together warm, sweet aniseed flavors and aromas with the fresh tartness of raspberry and a bite of sour lime.

INGREDIENTS

- 1 bottle Mocktails Mockapolitan
- ½ tsp. (1g) fennel seeds
- 1 star anise pod
- 8 fresh raspberries, plus more for garnish
- 1 tsp. (5ml) freshly squeezed lime juice
- Ice

METHOD

1. Add the fennel seeds, star anise, fresh raspberries, and lime juice to a cocktail shaker and muddle together to form a pulp.
2. Add ice to fill ⅓ of the shaker.
3. Add the entire bottle of Mockapolitan and shake vigorously for 5 to 8 seconds.
4. Strain into a martini glass and garnish with fresh raspberries.

MOCKTAIL BEVERAGES, INC.
BILL GAMELLI

Mocktail Beverages was founded in 2018 by former Wall Street Executive Bill Gamelli and his two co-founding partners, Mark Guthrie and Jim Dowla, to create healthy, sophisticated beverages for every guest at the party. They worked with global award-winning mixologist Ezra Star to create their first four flavors and continue to source and combine natural, sustainable, and ethically sourced botanicals to create complex, delicious drinks.

CHAPTER 2:
Traditional Mocktails and Mixed Drinks

Alcohol-free drinks have been around as long as we've had cocktail culture. The traditional-style mixed drinks in this chapter, whether blended, shaken, stirred, or built, are all based around classic cocktail design: mixing two or more ingredients and flavor elements to create festive, refreshing, and relaxing drinks. These drinks are perfect for parties big and small or quiet evenings at home.

Try this zesty Lime Rickey. Recipe on page 91.

I'll Fake Manhattan

The Manhattan is a classic cocktail that blends a variety of flavors. Enjoy as shown or try adding an alcohol-free whiskey to the mix.

INGREDIENTS

- 1 part cranberry juice
- 1 part fresh orange juice
- 1 dash aromatic bitters
- 1 dash maraschino cherry syrup or grenadine
- 1 dash lemon juice
- Ice cubes
- Maraschino cherry, for garnish

METHOD

1. Shake all ingredients in a cocktail shaker or stir with ice.
2. Strain into a chilled cocktail glass.
3. Garnish with a maraschino cherry.

What, Me Worry?

The Michelada is a favorite savory drink from Mexico. This drink draws on that heritage, but swaps in alcohol-free beer and lightens up the spice for true refreshment.

INGREDIENTS

- 1 glass alcohol-free beer
- 1 splash tomato juice or Bloody Mary mix
- Salt
- Lime wedge to garnish

METHOD

1. Combine the alcohol-free beer and tomato juice or Bloody Mary mix in a mug or salt-rimmed pint glass.
2. Garnish with the lime wedge.

Virgin Margarita

With their sour flavor and tequila kick, margaritas are always a party favorite. This alcohol-free version amps up the sweet and sour citrus flavors to create a true crowd-pleaser. **Note:** If you make this with a traditional sour mix (featuring egg white), pregnant women and the elderly should avoid drinking.

INGREDIENTS

- 3 parts sour mix
- 1 part lime cordial or lime juice
- 1 part fresh orange juice
- Crushed ice or ice cubes
- Lime wedge, for garnish

METHOD

1. Blend all ingredients or shake together in a cocktail shaker.
2. Serve in a salt-frosted margarita glass. If shaking in a cocktail shaker, strain carefully into the glass.
3. Garnish with a lime wedge.

Virgin Sea Breeze

This tangy and refreshing drink evokes dreams of warm tropical beaches.

INGREDIENTS

- 1 part cranberry juice
- 1 part grapefruit juice
- Ice cubes

METHOD

1. Fill a tall glass with ice cubes.
2. Pour the juices over the ice.
3. Stir gently and serve ungarnished.

Grenadine Rickey

This carbonated blend of sweet grenadine and sour lime is a perfect drink for hot summer evenings.

INGREDIENTS

- 1½ fl. oz. (45ml) grenadine
- 1½ fl. oz. (45ml) lime juice
- 1½ fl. oz. (45ml) soda water
- Ice cubes
- Lime wedge, for garnish

METHOD

1. Combine the grenadine and lime juice with ice in a tall glass.
2. Top up with the soda.
3. Garnish with the lime wedge.

Safe Sex on the Beach

The original Sex on the Beach cocktail is made with vodka and Midori liqueur. This version removes the alcohol, but it's still a sweet, tart, and sexy drink.

INGREDIENTS

- 1 part peach nectar
- 3 parts fresh orange juice
- 3 parts pineapple juice or grapefruit juice
- 1 squeeze fresh lime juice
- Ice cubes
- Fresh peach slice, for garnish

METHOD

1. Fill a tall glass with ice cubes.
2. Add juices in order.
3. Stir gently and garnish with a peach slice.

Virgin Mary

As the name suggests, this has all the spicy savory flavors of the ever-popular Bloody Mary without the need for vodka.

INGREDIENTS

- 1 can tomato juice
- 1 dash fresh lemon juice or lime juice
- 2 dashes Worcestershire sauce
- 2 drops Tabasco sauce
- Salt, pepper, and celery salt to taste
- Ice cubes
- Celery stalk, for garnish

METHOD

1. Shake all ingredients in a cocktail shaker.
2. Strain into your preferred glass and use the celery stick as a stirrer.

Unfuzzy Navel

Rather than using peach schnapps, freshen up this 1980s classic with crisp peaches.

INGREDIENTS

- 3 fl. oz. (90ml) fresh orange juice
- 1 fresh peach, cut into chunks
- 1 dash grenadine
- Ice cubes

METHOD

1. Blend the ingredients with ice until smooth.
2. Serve in a tall glass.

Honeymoon Cocktail

After all the champagne toasts at a wedding reception, the bride and groom (and maybe the guests) might benefit from something light and fresh.

INGREDIENTS

- 1 part apple juice
- 1 part fresh orange juice
- 1 squeeze fresh lime juice
- 2 tsp. (10ml) honey
- Crushed ice
- Orange peel and candied or maraschino cherries, for garnish

METHOD

1. Shake all ingredients in a cocktail shaker.
2. Strain the mixture into champagne flutes.
3. Garnish with a spiral of orange peel and cherries.

San Francisco

Here's a delightful tall drink for a hot summer evening featuring all the sweet and tangy citrus flavors. **Note:** If you make this with a traditional sour mix (featuring egg white) or choose to add the egg white separately, pregnant women and the elderly should avoid drinking. The drink can still be enjoyed without egg white but will lack some of the frothy texture.

INGREDIENTS

- 1 part fresh orange juice
- 1 part grapefruit juice
- 1 part pineapple juice
- 1 part sour mix or fresh lemon juice
- 1 egg white, optional
- 1 dash grenadine
- Ice cubes
- Soda water
- Candied/glacé cherries and orange slices, for garnish

METHOD

1. Place all ingredients except for soda water in a cocktail shaker and shake well.
2. Strain into a tall glass, filling it about halfway.
3. Top up with soda water and garnish with cherries and orange slices as desired.

Strawberry Daiquiri

The fresh strawberry flavor blends perfectly with the sour mix in this alcohol-free version of a classic bar favorite. **Note:** If you make this with a traditional sour mix (featuring egg white), pregnant women and the elderly should avoid drinking.

INGREDIENTS

- 3 oz. (85g) fresh or frozen strawberries
- 1 splash sour mix
- 1 dash grenadine
- Ice cubes
- Fresh fruit, for garnish

METHOD

1. Blend all ingredients until smooth.
2. Pour into your preferred glass and garnish with fresh fruit.

Cherry Pop

Good cocktails should look as good as they taste. This attractive drink has a good balance of sweet and sour, which you can adjust to suit your palate.

INGREDIENTS

- 2 parts cherry syrup
- 2 parts fresh orange juice
- 1 part fresh lemon juice
- Soda water
- 5 to 6 ice cubes
- Slice of lemon and a glacé cherry, for garnish

METHOD

1. Shake the syrup and juices with the ice cubes in a cocktail shaker.
2. Strain into a wine goblet, top up with soda water, and garnish with a slice of lemon and cherry to serve.

Fun-Gria

Sangria is usually made with red wine and orange juice. Replace the wine with red grape juice to lose the alcohol but keep the flavor.

INGREDIENTS

- 1 part fresh orange juice
- 1 part red grape juice
- 1 generous squeeze lemon juice
- Four ice cubes
- Orange zest
- Lemon slice, for garnish

METHOD

1. Place ice cubes in a cocktail shaker and add the juices. Shake well.
2. Strain into a sugar-frosted wine glass.
3. Sprinkle with orange zest and garnish with a lemon slice.

Saginaw Snooze

This popular alcohol-free cocktail is known to many bartenders around the world.

INGREDIENTS

- 3 fl. oz. (90ml) apple juice
- 3 fl. oz. (90ml) cranberry juice
- 1 tsp. (5ml) honey
- Lemon wheel and cinnamon stick, for garnish

METHOD

1. Heat the ingredients together in a small saucepan.
2. Pour into an Irish coffee mug.
3. Garnish with the lemon wheel and cinnamon stick.

Baby Buck

The Buck's Fizz is a popular traditional champagne brunch drink, similar to a Mimosa. There's no reason you can't replace the champagne with sparkling grape juice and add a little dryness with a dash of lime!

INGREDIENTS

- 1 part fresh orange juice
- 1 part sparkling white grape juice
- 1 squeeze fresh lime juice
- Twist of lemon rind, for garnish

METHOD

1. Pour the juices into a champagne flute.
2. Stir gently and garnish with the twist of lemon rind.

Virgin Piña Colada

Coconut cream may be difficult to find, but it will make all the difference for this perfect alcohol-free tropical delight.

INGREDIENTS

- 5 to 6 pineapple chunks
- 1 part pineapple juice
- Generous splash fresh orange juice
- 1 part coconut cream
- 1 Tbsp. (15ml) single/light cream
- Crushed ice
- Maraschino cherry and pineapple wedge, for garnish

METHOD

1. Add all ingredients to a blender; blend for about 10 seconds.
2. Strain into your preferred glass.
3. Garnish with a maraschino cherry and pineapple wedge, as desired.

Lemon Squash

A bubbly fresh lemon squash is the perfect drink to pair with a spring or summer picnic.

INGREDIENTS

- Lemon wedges
- 1 splash simple syrup
- Soda water
- Ice cubes

METHOD

1. Muddle the lemon wedges with the syrup in a tall glass.
2. Add the ice and top up with the soda water.

Saint Clements

This light citrus drink gets its name from the traditional English nursery rhyme, "Oranges and Lemons."

INGREDIENTS

- 1 part fresh orange juice
- 1 part sparkling bitter lemon
- Crushed ice
- Orange slices, for garnish

METHOD

1. Pour the orange juice over the crushed ice in a tall glass.
2. Top up with the bitter lemon and garnish with a slice or two of orange.

Pussyfoot

This citrus-based drink is supposedly an excellent cure for hangovers. Make sure the egg is very fresh. Drinks with raw egg are best avoided by pregnant women and the elderly.

INGREDIENTS

- 1 part fresh lemon juice
- 1 part fresh orange juice
- 1 part lime juice
- 1 splash grenadine
- 1 egg yolk
- 5 to 6 ice cubes
- Maraschino cherry, for garnish

METHOD

1. Place all ingredients in a cocktail shaker and shake well until the mixture is blended.
2. Strain into a chilled wine glass and garnish with a cherry.

Strawberry Colada

Strawberries brighten up this tropical holiday escape.

INGREDIENTS

- 1 part fresh or frozen strawberries
- 1 part cream of coconut
- 1 part pineapple juice
- Ice cubes
- Fresh fruit, for garnish

METHOD

1. Blend all the ingredients until smooth.
2. Pour into your preferred glass and garnish with fresh fruit.

Cinderella

This refreshing drink should ideally be drunk from a glass slipper, but they're not easy to find these days. **Note:** If you make this with a traditional sour mix (featuring egg white), pregnant women and the elderly should avoid drinking.

INGREDIENTS

- 1 part pineapple juice
- 1 part fresh lemon juice or sour mix
- 1 part fresh orange juice
- 1 dash grenadine
- 5 to 6 ice cubes
- Soda water
- Maraschino cherry or pineapple slice, for garnish

METHOD

1. Add all the ingredients except for the soda water into a cocktail shaker and shake well.
2. Strain into a tall glass.
3. Top up with soda water and garnish with a maraschino cherry or pineapple slice.

Cranberry Grape Cocktail

The slight tartness of cranberry juice is just enough to offset the sweetness of grape juice. Add the optional squeeze of lemon juice to the blend if the drink is too sweet for your palate.

INGREDIENTS

- 1 part cranberry juice
- 1 part white grape juice
- 1 squeeze lemon juice, optional
- Crushed ice
- Mint leaf, to garnish

METHOD

1. Pour the cranberry and grape juices, and the lemon juice, if using, over crushed ice in a champagne flute.
2. Stir well and garnish with a mint leaf.

Transfusion

This alcohol-free take on the famous golf club cocktail is still just as refreshing as the original summer picnic.

INGREDIENTS

- 3 fl. oz. (90ml) grape juice
- 6 fl. oz. (180ml) ginger ale
- 1 splash lime juice
- Ice cubes
- Lime wedge, for garnish

METHOD

1. Build the ingredients over ice in a tall glass.
2. Garnish with the lime wedge.

Rock Shandy

This is an old classic and a perfect drink for those occasions when you don't want alcohol but need to sip something refreshing. It's dry enough to appeal to adult tastes, and the dash of bitters gives it a sophisticated look.

INGREDIENTS

- 1 part soda water
- 1 part clear lemonade
- 2 dashes aromatic bitters
- 3 to 4 ice cubes
- Slice of lemon, for garnish

METHOD

1. Pour the soda water and lemonade over the ice in a tall glass.
2. Stir gently and add the bitters, allowing it to float near the top and create a band of pink.
3. Garnish with the lemon slice.

Pony's Neck

An alcohol-free version of a Horse's Neck, most claim this is better than the original!

INGREDIENTS

- 1 dash aromatic bitters
- 1 orange
- 1 lemon
- 1 dash lime cordial or lime juice
- Ginger ale
- Crushed ice
- Maraschino or candied/glacé cherry, for garnish

METHOD

1. Shake a dash of bitters into a tall glass and swirl to coat the sides.
2. Peel the orange to make a thin, unbroken spiral. Hook this over the edge of the glass, so that it forms a spiral into the glass.
3. Squeeze half the orange and the whole lemon into a separate glass, with a scoop of crushed ice.
4. Add the lime cordial and stir well.
5. Strain into the prepared glass and top with ginger ale.
6. Decorate with a cherry on a stick and serve.

Rosy Pippin

This carbonated drink mixes crisp apple freshness with tart sour mix for pure refreshment. **Note:** If you make this with a traditional sour mix (featuring egg white), pregnant women and the elderly should avoid drinking.

INGREDIENTS

- 4 fl. oz. (120ml) apple juice
- 1 splash grenadine
- 1 splash sour mix
- Ginger ale
- Ice cubes
- Apple slice, for garnish

METHOD

1. Shake the apple juice, grenadine, sour mix, and ice cubes in a cocktail shaker.
2. Pour into a tall glass.
3. Top with the ginger ale and garnish with the apple slice.

Shirley Temple

Named after the legendary child actress, this classic drink was originally designed for children, but it's so delicious, many adults have discovered they enjoy it too!

INGREDIENTS

- 1 splash grenadine
- Ginger ale or lemon-lime soda
- 1 squeeze fresh lime juice, optional
- Ice cubes
- Orange slice and maraschino cherry, for garnish

METHOD

1. Splash the grenadine over ice in a tall glass.
2. Top up with ginger ale or soda. If the drink is a bit too sweet, stir in a squeeze of fresh lime juice.
3. Garnish with a slice of orange and a cherry.

Lime Cola

Add a zing to regular cola with fresh lime juice.

INGREDIENTS

- Juice of 1 lime
- Cola
- Crushed ice or ice cubes, as desired
- Lime wedge, for garnish

METHOD

1. Build the ingredients over ice in a tall glass.
2. Stir gently and garnish with the lime wedge.

Down East Delight

This classic mocktail can be enjoyed as-is or mixed with your favorite alcohol-free spirit.

INGREDIENTS

- 1 part cranberry juice
- 1 part pineapple juice
- 1 part orange juice
- 1 dash simple syrup
- Ice cubes
- Maraschino cherry, for garnish

METHOD

1. Build the ingredients over ice in a tall glass.
2. Garnish with the cherry.

Lime Rickey

A "lime and soda" is one of the most popular alcohol-free cocktails. Add a fresh twist with a dash of grenadine.

INGREDIENTS

- 1 part lime cordial
- Soda water
- 1 dash grenadine
- Ice cubes
- Sprig of mint, for garnish

METHOD

1. Pour lime cordial over ice in a tall glass.
2. Top up with soda water, add grenadine, and stir gently.
3. Garnish with a sprig of mint.

Yankee Flip

This cocktail is normally made with red wine, but red grape juice gives a similar texture and flavor. Drinks with raw egg are best avoided by pregnant women and the elderly.

INGREDIENTS

- 1 egg yolk
- 1 tsp. (6g) caster sugar
- 1 part pineapple juice
- 2 parts red grape juice
- 5 to 6 ice cubes
- Grated nutmeg, for garnish

METHOD

1. Place all ingredients in a cocktail shaker until smoothly blended.
2. Strain into a wine glass and add a sprinkling of grated nutmeg to the top.

Cardinal Punch

This is a fruit-filled classic that is perfect for special events and lazy afternoons.

INGREDIENTS

- 1 part cranberry juice
- 1 part ginger ale
- 1 splash fresh orange juice
- 1 dash fresh lemon juice
- 1 dash simple syrup
- Ice cubes

METHOD

1. Build ingredients over ice in a tall glass.

The Limey

British sailors earned the nickname "limeys" because they were served regular doses of lime juice to combat scurvy during long ocean voyages. Drinks with raw egg are best avoided by pregnant women and the elderly.

INGREDIENTS

- 1 part fresh lemon juice
- 2 parts fresh lime juice
- 1 egg white
- 5 to 6 ice cubes
- Maraschino cherry, for garnish

METHOD

1. Shake the ingredients well in a cocktail shaker.
2. Strain into a martini glass and garnish with a cherry.

Parson's Particular

There are several alcohol-free drinks that suggest they should be served to parsons, reverends, or priests, presumably assuming that good clerics would not approve of strong drinks at the church festival. This drink is best avoided by pregnant women and the elderly.

INGREDIENTS

- 1 part fresh lemon juice
- 2 parts fresh orange juice
- 1 egg yolk
- 5 to 6 ice cubes
- 2 dashes grenadine
- Glacé cherry, for garnish

METHOD

1. Shake the juices, egg yolk, and ice together well in a cocktail shaker.
2. Strain into a wine glass and add the grenadine on top.
3. Garnish with the cherry.

Tomato Cooler

This savory, citrus refresher is perfect for breakfast or brunch.

INGREDIENTS

- 1 splash lemon juice
- Tomato juice, to fill
- 1 splash tonic
- Lemon wedge and celery stalk, for garnish

METHOD

1. Combine the juices in a tall glass.
2. Add the tonic and garnish with the lemon wedge and celery stalk.

Jungle Cooler

There are very few fruit juice combinations that don't go well together. This one was designed to capture the exotic character of the tropical jungle.

INGREDIENTS
- 4 parts pineapple juice
- 2 parts fresh orange juice
- 1 part passion fruit purée or cordial
- 1 part coconut milk
- Crushed ice
- Slice of pineapple, for garnish

METHOD
1. Shake the ingredients well in a cocktail shaker.
2. Strain into a tall glass and garnish with a slice of pineapple.

Pom-Pom

The egg white gives this pink drink a lovely silvery sheen and a topping of froth. Drinks with raw egg are best avoided by pregnant women and the elderly.

INGREDIENTS

- 1 egg white
- 1 tsp. (5ml) grenadine
- Juice of 1 large lemon
- Lemonade
- 6 ice cubes

METHOD

1. Add ice cubes, egg white, grenadine, and lemon juice to a cocktail shaker and shake well.
2. Strain into a tall glass, top up with lemonade, and stir gently.

Sunset Cooler

A sweet, cold drink to enjoy while watching a beautiful sunset.

INGREDIENTS

- 4 fl. oz. (120ml) cranberry juice
- 2½ fl. oz. (75ml) fresh orange juice
- 1 splash lemon juice
- Ginger ale
- Ice cubes
- Fresh fruit, for garnish

METHOD

1. Blend the juices with the ice and pour into a tall glass.
2. Top up with ginger ale and garnish with fresh fruit.

Lassie

Whether named after a Scottish girl or the famous movie dog, this is a popular classic among mocktails with a very appealing flavor.

INGREDIENTS

- 4 parts plain drinking yogurt
- 1 part heavy cream
- 2 tsp. (12g) caster sugar
- Ice cubes
- Glacé or maraschino cherry, for garnish

METHOD

1. Shake all ingredients vigorously in a cocktail shaker.
2. Strain into a martini glass or wine goblet and garnish with a cherry.

Lime Cooler

When you're looking for a cool, refreshing drink without the sweetness, this could be the one.

INGREDIENTS

- 1 Tbsp. (15ml) lime juice
- Tonic water
- Ice cubes
- Slice of lime, for garnish

METHOD

1. Pour the lime juice over the ice cubes in a tall glass.
2. Top up with tonic water, stir gently, and garnish with the lime slice.

Roy Rogers

This famous drink is a simple and refreshing soda fountain classic!

INGREDIENTS

- Cola, to fill
- 1 splash grenadine
- Ice cubes
- Orange wheel and maraschino cherry, for garnish

METHOD

1. Build the ingredients over ice in a tall glass.
2. Garnish with the orange wheel and cherry.

Blue Spark

There are few things as dramatic—or unexpected—as a blue drink.

INGREDIENTS

- ½ tsp. (2.5ml) blue food coloring
- 2 dashes aromatic bitters
- 1 part lychee juice
- 3 parts fizzy lemonade
- Crushed ice
- Slice of lemon, for garnish

METHOD

1. Place crushed ice into a tall mixing glass and add all ingredients.
2. Stir gently to avoid losing the fizz.
3. Strain into a tall glass and garnish with a slice of lemon

Cairns Cooler

This fruity drink, which originated in Australia, has a distinctive tropical flavor.

INGREDIENTS

- 1 part pineapple juice
- 1 part fresh orange juice
- ½ part coconut cream
- 1 bar measure simple syrup
- 6 ice cubes
- Thin slice of pineapple and maraschino cherry, for garnish

METHOD

1. Shake all ingredients well in a cocktail shaker.
2. Strain into a tall glass and garnish with the pineapple slice and cherry.

Sonoma Nouveau

Using alcohol-free versions of beer, wine, or spirits will let you mix drinks that have flavor profiles very similar to those of traditional cocktails.

INGREDIENTS

- 5 fl. oz. (150ml) alcohol-free white wine
- Soda water
- Cranberry juice
- Ice cubes
- Twist of lemon, for garnish

METHOD

1. Pour the wine over ice into a tall glass and add the soda to almost full.
2. Float the cranberry juice on top and garnish with the twist of lemon.

Strawberry Must

This unexpected blend of creamy, sweet, and acidic flavors will keep your guests on their toes.

INGREDIENTS

- 2 handfuls strawberries, hulled
- 2 tsp. (10ml) balsamic vinegar
- 3 fl. oz. (90ml) cream
- Honey, to taste
- 1 to 2 ice cubes

METHOD

1. Blend the strawberries until smooth.
2. Pour in the balsamic vinegar, cream, and honey to taste. Serve over ice.

Parson's Pleasure

Here's another drink designed to please spiritual leaders. This one is similar to the Parson's Particular, but is made as a taller drink. Drinks with raw egg are best avoided by pregnant women and the elderly.

INGREDIENTS

- 1 egg yolk
- Juice of 1 large orange
- 4 dashes grenadine
- Soda water
- 5 to 6 ice cubes
- Twist of lemon rind, for garnish

METHOD

1. Shake ice, egg yolk, orange juice, and grenadine well in a cocktail shaker.
2. Strain into a tall glass.
3. Top up with soda water, stir gently, and garnish with the lemon twist.

Johnny Appleseed

Liven up these breakfast-favorite fruit juices to create a brunch-ready mixed drink.

INGREDIENTS

- 2 fl. oz. (60ml) apple juice
- 1 splash fresh orange juice
- 1 splash soda water
- Ice cubes

METHOD

1. Blend the ingredients with ice until smooth.
2. Serve in a champagne glass.

Grape Sparkler

This is an attractive drink to serve in the fall when grapes are plentiful. This recipe is reminiscent of champagne with crisp sparkling white grape juice.

INGREDIENTS

- 2 whole white grapes
- 2 whole black grapes
- 1 squeeze lemon juice
- Sparkling white grape juice

METHOD

1. Thread white and black grapes alternately on a long cocktail stick and stand it upright in a champagne flute.
2. Squeeze lemon juice over the grapes and fill the glass with sparkling white grape juice.

Grape Crush

We are fortunate these days to be able to buy a wide range of pure fruit juices in cartons, cans, or bottles, so fruit-based drinks can be enjoyed all year round. **Note:** If you make this with a traditional sour mix (featuring egg white), pregnant women and the elderly should avoid drinking.

INGREDIENTS

- 3 parts grape juice
- 1 part cranberry juice
- 1 part sour mix
- Lemonade
- Crushed ice

METHOD

1. Pour the grape juice, cranberry juice, and sour mix over ice into a wine glass.
2. Top up with lemonade and serve.

Ginger Snap

Anybody who enjoys ginger beer will appreciate the flick of ginger heat in this unusual drink. If you can't find ginger marmalade, you can substitute lime marmalade and add a little more ginger.

INGREDIENTS

- 1 part fresh orange juice
- 1 part grapefruit juice
- 1 part cranberry juice
- 2 tsp. (10ml) ginger marmalade
- ½ tsp. (3g) ground ginger or fresh grated ginger root
- Slice of orange, for garnish
- Crushed ice

METHOD

1. Shake all ingredients well in a cocktail
2. Strain into a tall glass and garnish with a slice of orange.

Heaven Scent

This drink blends the exotic sweetness of lychees with the more traditional rosewater to create something that's completely different.

INGREDIENTS

- 8 lychees, peeled
- 1 tsp. (5ml) rosewater
- 2 to 3 ice cubes
- 1 tsp. (5ml) grenadine

METHOD

1. Blend the lychees with the rosewater and ice.
2. Pour in grenadine.

Nicholas

This sweet and sour drink is another one that's perfect for brunch or a sunny summer afternoon. **Note:** If you make this with a traditional sour mix (featuring egg white), pregnant women and the elderly should avoid drinking.

INGREDIENTS

- 1 splash grapefruit juice
- 1 splash fresh orange juice
- 1 splash sour mix
- 1 dash grenadine
- Ice cubes

METHOD

1. Shake all the ingredients together in a cocktail shaker.
2. Pour over ice in a tall glass.

Island Romance

This drink combines tropical flavors in an attractive blend. Try to float each ingredient gently on top of the previous one for a dramatic effect.

INGREDIENTS

- 1 slice fresh, ripe honeydew melon, peeled and cut into chunks
- Juice of 1 large orange
- 1 part coconut milk
- 1 part mango juice
- Crushed ice
- Whipped cream, for garnish

METHOD

1. Blend honeydew with ice to a purée.
2. Place purée carefully into a champagne flute, filling it to about one third.
3. Float the coconut milk on top of it, followed by the orange and mango juices, trying to keep them separate.
4. Top with whipped cream.

Cranberry Sparkler

Cranberry juice is a popular tangy fruit drink, sweet but with just enough acidity to make it exciting.

INGREDIENTS

- 1 part cranberry juice
- 1 part fresh lemon juice
- 1 part soda water
- Slice of lemon, for garnish
- Crushed ice

METHOD

1. Pour the ingredients over ice in a tall glass.
2. Stir gently and garnish with a slice of lemon.

Miami Vice

This sweet, creamy cola and root beer mix is an unexpected mix that's perfect for family picnics.

INGREDIENTS

- 2 fl. oz. (60ml) half-and-half
- 2 fl. oz. (60ml) root beer
- 1 squeeze chocolate syrup
- Cola, to fill
- ice cubes

METHOD

1. Shake all the ingredients, except the cola, in a cocktail shaker.
2. Pour into a tall glass and top up with the cola.

Grecian Lady

This is one of those fruit-based drinks that can be decorated with any fresh fruit that's in season. It looks exotic and tastes wonderful.

INGREDIENTS

- 4 parts peach juice
- 2 parts fresh orange juice
- 1 part fresh lemon juice
- Soda water
- Fruit slices or stoned cherries, for garnish
- Crushed ice

METHOD

1. Shake the juices with ice in a cocktail shaker.
2. Strain into a large wine glass.
3. Add a squirt of soda water to fill the glass and garnish with slices of fruit or cherries threaded on a cocktail stick.

Surfers' Paradise

This is the perfect summer drink, originally designed to be enjoyed after an exhilarating session in the waves, but why wait until the surf is up?

INGREDIENTS

- Juice of 1 fresh lime
- 2 dashes aromatic bitters
- Lemonade
- Crushed ice
- Slice of orange, for garnish

METHOD

1. Pour the lime juice, bitters, and lemonade over ice in a tall glass.
2. Stir gently and garnish with a slice of orange.

Montego Bay

This is a fizzy tropical beverage to accompany perfect poolside days. **Note:** If you make this with a traditional sour mix (featuring egg white), pregnant women and the elderly should avoid drinking.

INGREDIENTS

- 2 fl. oz. (60ml) fresh orange juice
- 2 fl. oz. (60ml) sour mix
- 1 splash grenadine
- Soda water (to fill)
- Ice cubes
- Fresh fruit, for garnish

METHOD

1. Shake all the ingredients, except the soda, with ice.
2. Pour into a tall glass and top up with the soda.
3. Garnish with fresh fruit.

Dry Grape Cocktail

For a drink that's not sickly sweet, try this elegant cocktail. The grenadine adds color and can be used to adjust the sweetness to taste.

INGREDIENTS

- 2 parts white grape juice
- 1 part fresh lemon juice
- 1 splash grenadine
- Crushed ice

METHOD

1. Shake all ingredients well in a cocktail shaker.
2. Strain into a cocktail glass.

Plum Joy

Using fresh fruit or freshly squeezed juice always adds to the flavor of a drink. Canned or preserved fruit products are fine, but they often lack the pure tang of fresh fruit.

INGREDIENTS

- 2 large, very ripe plums, peeled and cut into small pieces
- Crushed ice
- Cold water
- Juice of ½ lemon
- 2 Tbsp. (30ml) simple syrup
- 2 Tbsp. (30ml) plum jam
- Sparkling bitter lemon

METHOD

1. Place plums in a blender with a scoop of crushed ice, a couple spoons of cold water, lemon juice, simple syrup, and plum jam and blend to a smooth purée.
2. Strain the mixture into a tall glass and top up with the bitter lemon.
3. Stir gently to blend.

A.S. Macpherson

Bitters and orange are a perfect sophisticated mix. Adding soda water adds lightness to create a refreshing dinner drink. **Note:** If you make this with a traditional sour mix (featuring egg white), pregnant women and the elderly should avoid drinking.

INGREDIENTS

- 3 to 4 dashes aromatic bitters
- 1 splash sour mix
- 1 splash fresh orange juice
- Soda water, to fill
- Ice cubes
- Fresh fruit, for garnish

METHOD

1. Shake all the ingredients, except the soda, in a cocktail shaker.
2. Strain into a tall glass over fresh ice.
3. Top up with the soda and garnish with fresh fruit.

Cranberry Cooler

This is a slightly different version of the Cranberry Sparkler (see page 108), using lime cordial instead of lemon juice, and ginger ale instead of soda water.

INGREDIENTS

- 1 part cranberry juice
- 1 splash lime cordial
- 1 part ginger ale
- Slice of lemon, for garnish
- Crushed ice

METHOD

1. Pour the cranberry juice, lime cordial, and ginger ale over crushed ice in a tall glass.
2. Stir gently and garnish with a slice of lemon.

Fizzy Lemonade

One of the oldest and most popular drinks around, this mix is refreshing without being cloyingly sweet.

INGREDIENTS

- Juice of 1 large lemon
- 2 tsp. (12g) caster sugar
- Soda water
- Ice cubes
- Slice of lemon, for garnish

METHOD

1. Pour the lemon juice into a tall glass, add the sugar, and stir until it has dissolved.
2. Top up with soda water and add a few ice cubes.
3. Stir gently and garnish with a slice of lemon.

Orangeade

If you're looking for a sweet treat to accompany breakfast or brunch, this drink is for you.

INGREDIENTS

- 1 part fresh orange juice
- 1 part soda water
- 1 splash simple syrup
- Ice cubes
- Orange wheel, for garnish

METHOD

1. Build over ice in a tall glass.
2. Garnish with the orange wheel.

Silver Sour

The egg whites give this little drink a nice gloss and the lemon juice provides a tangy balance to the sweetness of the apricot juice. Drinks with raw egg are best avoided by pregnant women and the elderly.

INGREDIENTS

- 1 egg white
- Ice cubes
- Juice of 1 large lemon
- 1 part thick apricot juice or purée
- 1 tsp. (6g) caster sugar
- Soda water
- 2 slices green apple, for garnish

METHOD

1. Shake the egg white, ice cubes, lemon juice, apricot juice or purée, and caster sugar well in a cocktail shaker for about 10 seconds.
2. Strain into a wine goblet and top up with soda water.
3. Stir gently and garnish with a couple of slices of apple on the rim of the glass.

Royal Fizz

The original cocktail of this name contains raspberry brandy. This drink switches it up with raspberry syrup instead. A perfect drink for a hot summer's day.

INGREDIENTS

- 1 part fresh orange juice
- 1 part lime cordial
- 1 part raspberry syrup
- Soda water
- Cracked ice

METHOD

1. Place a small scoop of cracked ice in a cocktail shaker and add the orange juice, lime cordial, and raspberry syrup.
2. Shake well and strain into a tall glass.
3. Top up with chilled soda water and serve with a straw.

Pac Man

This gingery sweet citrus drink offers a fresh take on everyone's favorite traditional cocktail ingredients.

INGREDIENTS

- 1 dash aromatic bitters
- 1 dash grenadine
- 1 splash lemon juice
- Ginger ale, to fill
- Ice cubes
- Orange wheel, for garnish

METHOD

1. Stir all the ingredients, except the ginger ale, with the ice.
2. Pour into a tall glass and fill with the ginger ale.
3. Garnish with the orange wheel.

Red Currant and Lemon Delight

Red currant jelly is a popular traditional English ingredient, often accompanying Sunday roast dinners. This drink takes what many might view as an old-fashioned ingredient and freshens it up with a little imagination.

INGREDIENTS

- 2 Tbsp. (30ml) red currant jelly
- Boiling water
- 4 to 5 ice cubes
- Juice of 2 lemons
- Soda water
- Slice of lemon, for garnish

METHOD

1. Place the red currant jelly in a cup, add an equal quantity of boiling water, and stir until dissolved.
2. Pour the lemon juice over ice cubes in a tall glass.
3. Add the dissolved jelly.
4. Top up with soda water and garnish with a slice of lemon.

Southern Belle

The American South is the home of the Mint Julep. This is the version originally designed for the younger members of a Southern family—it's a Julep without the alcohol.

INGREDIENTS

- 2 sprigs mint leaves
- 1 tsp. (6g) caster sugar
- 1 generous squeeze lemon juice
- Ice cubes
- Ginger ale

METHOD

1. Place a sprig of mint in the bottom of a tall glass, add the sugar, and use a long-handled spoon to muddle the two together to extract as much mint flavor as possible.
2. Add a squeeze of lemon juice, a few ice cubes, and top up with ginger ale.
3. Garnish with the other sprig of mint and a decorative straw.

Beach Blanket Bingo

This tart blend of grapefruit and cranberry is perfect for hot days on the beach.

INGREDIENTS

- 1 part cranberry juice
- 1 part grapefruit juice
- Soda water, to fill
- Ice cubes
- Lime wedge, for garnish

METHOD

1. Stir the juices with ice in a tall glass and top up with the soda.
2. Garnish with the lime wedge.

Horse Feathers

For those who prefer a savory drink rather than a sweet one, this oddly named classic could become a favorite. It can even be served as a starter for a summer meal.

INGREDIENTS

- Clear beef consommé, cooled and chilled
- 1 dash Tabasco sauce
- 1 dash Worcestershire sauce
- 1 pinch salt
- 1 squeeze lemon juice
- 4 to 5 ice cubes
- Celery stick, for garnish

METHOD

1. Pour the consommé over ice cubes in a mixing glass and add the Tabasco and Worcestershire sauces, a pinch of salt, and the lemon juice to taste.
2. Stir well and strain into a large wine glass.
3. Garnish with a celery stick, which can double as a stirrer.

Appleade

This is a pleasant summer drink with subtle flavors that can be made a day or two ahead of time and set aside in the fridge until needed.

INGREDIENTS

- 2 large green apples, cut into small cubes
- Boiling water, enough to cover the apple cubes
- 1 Tbsp. (15g) brown sugar
- Crushed ice
- 1 pinch ground cinnamon
- Slice of apple, for garnish

METHOD

1. Place the apple pieces in a bowl and pour the boiling water over them.
2. Add the sugar and stir to dissolve.
3. Leave to cool, then strain and chill the liquid until needed. Discard the apple pieces.
4. To serve, fill a cocktail glass with crushed ice, pour the appleade over it, dust lightly with ground cinnamon, and garnish with a slice of apple.

Snow Queen

This easy-to-make short drink is very attractive and has a nice sharpness to it. The egg white gives it a silvery froth, so it requires no garnish to make it look pretty. Drinks with raw egg are best avoided by pregnant women and the elderly.

INGREDIENTS

- 1 egg white
- 1 generous dash lime cordial
- Lemonade
- 5 ice cubes

METHOD

1. Place five ice cubes in a cocktail shaker and add the egg white and a splash of lime cordial.
2. Shake very well and strain into a cocktail glass.
3. Carefully top up with lemonade, allowing the froth from the egg white to float on top.

Malibu Cooler

This is a slightly nutty, creamy tropical drink designed to sweeten up summer days.

INGREDIENTS

- 1 cup (240ml) pineapple juice
- 1 Tbsp. (15g) ground almonds
- 2 Tbsp. (30ml) coconut milk
- 3 ice cubes

METHOD

1. Stir the almonds and coconut milk with the pineapple juice.
2. Pour over ice.

Orange 'n' Bitters

Drinks do not have to be complicated to be good. This one simply uses the tangy bitterness of aromatic bitters to add a new dimension to plain fresh orange juice.

INGREDIENTS

- 2 dashes aromatic bitters
- 1 glass chilled fresh orange juice
- Crushed ice
- Sprig of mint, for garnish

METHOD

1. Fill a tall glass with crushed ice, add a couple dashes of bitters, and fill with orange juice.
2. Garnish with a sprig of mint and serve with a straw.

Kiddie Cocktail

Although called a Kiddie Cocktail, this sweet and sour blend of flavors will work for all ages. **Note:** If you make this with a traditional sour mix (featuring egg white), pregnant women and the elderly should avoid drinking.

INGREDIENTS

- 1 splash grenadine
- 1 splash sour mix
- Ice cubes
- Orange wheel and maraschino cherry, for garnish

METHOD

1. Shake the ingredients in a cocktail shaker.
2. Pour into a tall glass and garnish with orange wheel and cherry.

Sober Moment

This is a classic blend of flavors, with the slightly bitter tonic water balancing the other sweet tastes.

INGREDIENTS

- 1 part fresh orange juice
- 1 part fresh lime juice
- 1 splash grenadine
- Tonic water
- Ice cubes
- Twist of lime rind, for garnish

METHOD

1. Pour the orange and lime juices over ice in a tall glass and trickle the splash of grenadine over it.
2. Top up with tonic water and garnish with a twist of lime.

Jones Beach Cocktail

This savory drink uses lemon juice to balance the saltiness of the beef consommé.

INGREDIENTS

- 1 cup (240ml) beef consommé, cooled
- ½ cup (120ml) clam juice
- Juice of ½ lemon or lime
- ½ tsp. (2.5ml) horseradish sauce
- 2 dashes Worcestershire sauce
- Celery salt
- Crushed ice
- 2 ice cubes
- Sprig of parsley, to garnish

METHOD

1. Shake all the ingredients in a cocktail shaker until well mixed.
2. Place two ice cubes in a tall glass and strain the blended drink over them.
3. Garnish with a sprig of parsley.

Pearls and Lace

At first glance, this combination doesn't seem like it would work, but the sweetness of the cola, the citrus flavors, and the bitterness of the root beer make for a surprisingly delightful drink.

INGREDIENTS

- 2 fl. oz. (60ml) orange soda
- 2 fl. oz. (60ml) cola
- 2 fl. oz. (60ml) root beer
- 2 fl. oz. (60ml) 7UP
- 1 splash lemonade
- Ice cubes

METHOD

1. Build over ice in a tall glass.

The Keelplate

This is a coastal variation of the classic Bloody Mary, adding the unusual ingredient of clam juice.

INGREDIENTS

- 2 parts tomato juice
- 1 part clam juice
- 1 dash Worcestershire sauce
- 1 pinch celery salt
- Crushed ice
- Spring of mint leaves, for garnish

METHOD

1. Shake the ingredients well in a cocktail shaker.
2. Strain into a large wine glass and garnish with mint leaves.

Grape Spritzer

White grape juice is always
refreshing and the addition of the
light perfume of elderflower cordial
takes this drink to another level
of sophistication.

INGREDIENTS

- 1 cup (240ml) white grape juice
- 1 tsp. (5ml) elderflower cordial
- 6 fl. oz. (180 ml) sparkling mineral water
- 3 ice cubes
- Small bunch of grapes, for garnish

METHOD

1. Pour the white grape juice into a mixing
   glass and gently stir in the elderflower
   cordial and water.
2. Pour over ice and garnish with a small
   bunch of grapes.

Very Lemony Ade

This is a deliciously refreshing drink for those who like their lemonade with more lemon sourness and less sweetness. **Note:** If you make this with a traditional sour mix (featuring egg white), pregnant women and the elderly should avoid drinking.

INGREDIENTS

- 1 generous splash sour mix
- 1 part soda water
- 1 part sparkling bitter lemon
- Ice cubes
- Twist of lemon, for garnish

METHOD

1. Fill a tall glass with ice cubes and pour the sour mix over them.
2. Add the soda water and bitter lemon in equal quantities to fill the glass.
3. Stir gently and garnish with a twist of lemon. Serve with a straw.

Catherine Blossom

This drink originates in Canada, where maple syrup is widely used as a sweetener. It has a delightfully fresh taste.

INGREDIENTS

- Juice of 2 fresh oranges
- Juice of ½ small lemon
- 2 large spoons maple syrup
- Crushed ice
- Twist of lemon peel, for garnish

METHOD

1. Place the ingredients in a blender and blend well.
2. Strain into a wine goblet and garnish with a twist of lemon peel.

Mexican Sunset

This is an alcohol-free variation of the traditional Tequila Sunset, which obviously relies on fiery tequila for its kick.

INGREDIENTS

- Juice of 2 oranges
- 1 Tbsp. (15ml) grenadine
- Ice cubes
- Chunk of pineapple and a glacé cherry, for garnish

METHOD

1. Fill a wine glass or rocks glass with ice cubes and pour the orange juice over them.
2. Carefully float the grenadine on top of it, trying to keep the colors separate.
3. Garnish with a chunk of pineapple and a cherry on a cocktail stick.

Missionary

This drink calls to mind missionaries encountering the fresh flavors of tropical islands. **Note:** If you make this with a traditional sour mix (featuring egg white), pregnant women and the elderly should avoid drinking.

INGREDIENTS

- 2 fl. oz. (60ml) pineapple juice
- 1 fl. oz. (30ml) simple syrup
- 1 fl. oz. (30ml) sour mix
- Ice cubes
- Pineapple wedges and maraschino cherry, for garnish

METHOD

1. Shake all the ingredients together in a cocktail shaker.
2. Strain over fresh ice in a tall glass and garnish with the pineapple wedge and cherry.

Virgin Lea

This classic cocktail expertly combines a range of flavors. You'll find sweetness, tangy sharpness, and some spice.

INGREDIENTS

- ½ yellow pepper, seeds removed and cut into small slices
- 2 parts tomato juice
- 1 part passion fruit juice or cordial
- 1 tsp. (5ml) runny honey
- 2 dashes Worcestershire sauce
- Crushed ice
- Cherry tomato, for garnish

METHOD

1. Place the ingredients in a blender and blend thoroughly until the mixture is quite smooth.
2. Strain into a short glass and garnish with a cherry tomato on a stick.

CHAPTER 3:
Unusual Mixers and Drink Bases

The juices and teas in this chapter are delicious and satisfying on their own, but they will also work great as mixers for the abundance of alcohol-free spirits, botanicals, wines, and beers available on the market. See Mixing Alcohol-Free Cocktails, page 30. Feel confident exploring mixology by pairing these delicious and unexpected bases with various herbs, shrubs, syrups, and spices.

Try
this bright
Lavender
Lemonade.
Recipe on
page 135.

Summer Breeze

This drink combines three delicious fruit flavors: acidic citrus, sweet grape, and light earthy pear.

INGREDIENTS

- 1 part orange juice
- 1 part grape juice
- 1 part pear juice
- Ice cubes
- Twist of lime, for garnish

METHOD

1. Combine the juices together.
2. Pour into a glass over ice and garnish with a twist of lime.

Cherry Delight

This unusual mix of fruit juices works well on its own or with your favorite alcohol-free spirit.

INGREDIENTS

- 1 part apple juice
- 1 part pear juice
- 1 part cherry juice
- Ice cubes
- Fresh mint sprig, for garnish

METHOD

1. Combine the juices together.
2. Pour into a glass over ice and garnish with a mint sprig.

Grape Surprise

A celebration blending different grape flavors with a surprise pop of apple and mint. You can also lengthen this drink with sparkling mineral water for a light, refreshing beverage.

INGREDIENTS

- 1 part grape juice
- 1 part white grape juice
- 1 part apple
- 6 fresh mint leaves
- Ice cubes or crushed ice

METHOD

1. Combine the juices together.
2. Stir in the mint leaves and pour into a glass over ice.

In the Pink

This drink is as beautiful as it is refreshing and should add interest to any summer brunch, whether alcohol-free spirits are mixed in or not.

INGREDIENTS

- 1 part pink grapefruit juice
- 1 part cranberry juice
- 1 part apple
- Ice cubes or crushed ice

METHOD

1. Combine the juices together.
2. Pour into a glass over ice and serve chilled.

Just Peachy

This is a lovely fruit-filled drink that will charm guests at any event with its bold colors and textures and the beautiful floral garnish.

INGREDIENTS

- 1 part mandarin orange or blood orange juice
- 1 part peach juice or nectar
- Seeds of 1 pomegranate
- Borage flowers, for garnish

METHOD

1. Combine the juices.
2. Pour into glasses and drop in the pomegranate seeds.
3. Float a few borage flowers on top of each serving for a pretty final flourish.

Fruit Cup

This drink can be made as a single cocktail, but you can mix larger amounts of each ingredient in to make a large fruit punch for a party.

INGREDIENTS

- 1 part fresh orange juice
- 1 part grapefruit juice
- 1 part pineapple juice
- 1 part apple juice
- Ice cubes
- Slices of fresh fruit, to garnish

METHOD

1. Shake the juices and ice cubes well in a cocktail shaker.
2. Strain into a tall glass and garnish with fresh fruit slices and a colorful straw.

Guava Buzz

Guava has a delightful flavor and can be mixed with other juices and alcohol-free spirits to create some equally delightful drinks.

INGREDIENTS

- 1 part guava juice or nectar
- 1 part apricot juice
- 1 part pear juice
- Crushed ice

METHOD

1. Combine all the juices.
2. Pour into a glass over crushed ice.

Lavender Lemonade

This upmarket twist on traditional lemonade looks as good as it tastes. This recipe makes approximately 8 servings, so it's great for a spring or summer celebration!

INGREDIENTS

- 8 cups (1.9L) water
- 1 cup (200g) sugar
- 1½ cups (360ml) juice from a Meyer lemon
- 10 sprigs fresh lavender
- Sprigs of fresh lavender and lemon wheel, for garnish

METHOD

1. Boil water, add sugar, and simmer on low heat for five to seven minutes, stirring often.
2. When the sugar is dissolved, remove from heat and add lemon juice and lavender.
3. Let the lemonade cool to room temperature, remove the lavender sprigs, and refrigerate overnight.
4. Serve in your favorite glasses, garnished with sprigs of fresh lavender and lemon wheels.

Suspended Passion

This creamy beverage is perfect for breakfast or brunch or as a light afternoon treat.

INGREDIENTS

- 1 cup (240ml) fresh orange juice
- 1 banana, peeled and cut into chunks
- Pulp of 1 passion fruit

METHOD

1. Blend the orange juice with the banana.
2. Stir in the passion fruit pulp.

Sunny Morning

This icy fruit-filled beverage is sure to start your morning off right. Enjoy in the evening topped up with soda water or a light alcohol-free spirit or botanical.

INGREDIENTS

- 3 ice cubes
- 1 pear, peeled, halved, cored, and chopped
- 3 apricots, halved, stoned, and chopped
- 1 nectarine, halved, stoned, and chopped
- 3½ fl. oz. (105ml) pear juice
- Extra sliced apricot and nectarine to garnish

METHOD

1. Place the ice cubes in the blender and whiz, then add the rest of the ingredients and blend until smooth.
2. Pour into a glass and garnish with sliced apricot and nectarine.

Pink Lady

This is a simple drink blending sweet, sour, and tart flavors to create a refreshing mix that can be enjoyed on its own or combined with other ingredients.

INGREDIENTS

- 1 part red grapefruit juice
- 1 part white grapefruit juice
- 1 part cranberry juice

METHOD

1. Mix the juices together.

Red Silk

This is a sweet, tart blend that can be served alone or with other mixers to create a beverage that is smooth as silk.

INGREDIENTS

- 3 oz. (85g) strawberries, hulled and chopped
- 3 oz. (85g) raspberries
- 3 oz. (85g) blackberries
- 5 fl. oz. (150ml) apple juice
- Crushed ice to serve
- Extra raspberries and blackberries, for garnish

METHOD

1. Place all fruits and juice in the blender and blend until smooth.
2. Pour into a glass over ice and garnish with raspberries and blackberries.

Watermelon Wonder

This blend of sweet refreshing watermelon with bright lime and fresh rosemary is an unexpected combination to elevate your day.

INGREDIENTS

- 1 lb. (450g) watermelon, peeled, deseeded, and cut into chunks
- 1 lime, peeled and halved
- 1 sprig fresh rosemary, needles only
- Ice cubes to serve
- 1 watermelon wedge and fresh rosemary, for garnish

METHOD

1. Place the watermelon, lime, and rosemary in the blender and blend until smooth.
2. Pour into a glass over ice cubes and garnish with a chunk of watermelon and fresh rosemary.

Pineapple Pleasure

This is a minty and refreshingly light tropical beverage.

INGREDIENTS

- 4 ice cubes
- 1 pear, peeled, quartered, and cored
- ½ medium-sized pineapple, peeled, cored and eyes removed, and flesh cut into chunks
- 8 large fresh mint leaves, plus extra for garnish

METHOD

1. Place the ice cubes in the blender and whiz, then add the rest of the ingredients and blend until smooth.
2. Pour into a glass and garnish with mint.

Melon Magic

This drink base is a true green machine, loaded with tons of fruit and flavor.

INGREDIENTS

- 12 oz. (340g) honeydew melon, peeled, deseeded, and cut into chunks
- 2 kiwi fruits, peeled and quartered
- 4 lychees, peeled and stoned
- Extra kiwi fruit, for garnish

METHOD

1. Place all ingredients in the blender and blend until smooth.
2. Pour into a glass and serve chilled, garnished with kiwi fruit.

Berry Banana Blast

Berries and bananas are always a delicious pair, and the added apple juice brings an additional layer of flavor to this mix.

INGREDIENTS

- 5 oz. (142g) blackberries
- 5 oz. (142g) blueberries
- 1 banana, peeled and cut into chunks
- 8 fl. oz. (240ml) apple juice
- Ice cubes to serve
- Extra blackberries and blueberries, for garnish

METHOD

1. Place the fruits and juice in the blender and blend until smooth.
2. Pour into a glass over ice and garnish.

Pick-Me-Up

This minty citrus drink is sure to wake you up after a long, tiring day of work.

INGREDIENTS

- 2 oranges, peeled
- 8 fresh mint leaves
- 1 lime, peeled
- Pulp of 1 passion fruit

METHOD

1. Juice the oranges, mint, and lime together.
2. Stir in the passion fruit pulp and serve with a sprig of mint.

True Blue

This mix of dark vibrant berries creates a beautiful drink. If you want a thicker beverage, try using a juicer to create your own juices from the fresh fruits.

INGREDIENTS

- 1 part apple juice
- 1 part blackcurrant juice
- 1 part blueberry juice
- 1 part blackberry juice
- Ice cubes

METHOD

1. Combine the juices together and pour into glasses over ice.

Berry Dazzler

Drinks made with this fruit blend are sure to live up to the name and dazzle your guests.

INGREDIENTS

- 4 ice cubes
- 5 oz. (141g) cranberries
- 5 oz. (141g) blueberries
- 3½ fl. oz. (105ml) pear juice
- Extra cranberries and blueberries, for garnish

METHOD

1. Place the ice cubes in the blender and whiz.
2. Add the rest of the ingredients and blend until smooth.
3. Pour into a glass and serve chilled, garnished with extra cranberries and blueberries.

Fantasia

This drink is another perfect base for a tropical cocktail. This would work particularly well served by the pool.

INGREDIENTS

- 5 strawberries, rinsed and hulled
- Slice of honeydew melon, rind removed and cut into chunks
- 1 part fresh orange juice
- 1 part pineapple juice
- Crushed ice
- Thin slice of pineapple and 1 fresh strawberry, for garnish

METHOD

1. Place the strawberries, the melon, and the orange and pineapple juices in a blender and blend to a smooth consistency.
2. Place the crushed ice in a tall glass and pour the blended mixture over it.
3. Garnish with the remaining strawberry, sliced in half, and a slice of pineapple.

Tuscan Nectar

Figs provide the standout flavor in this beautiful drink that calls to mind a late Tuscan sunset.

INGREDIENTS

- 1 part grape juice
- 1 part fig juice
- Juice of ½ lemon

METHOD

1. Combine the grape and fig juices.
2. Stir in the lemon juice.

Berry Nice

This is another one of those mixers that will look beautiful and taste delicious on its own, but can easily be turned into a taller or more sophisticated drink with soda water or other ingredients.

INGREDIENTS

- 4 oz. (113g) strawberries
- 4 oz. (113g) raspberries
- 4 oz. (113g) blackberries
- 4 oz. (113g) blueberries
- A few extra berries, for garnish

METHOD

1. Blend all the berries together. Pour into glasses and serve garnished with extra fruits.

In the Mood

This drink is delicious and the sliced fresh fig as a garnish will work for the basic beverage or if you blend this base with other mixers.

INGREDIENTS

- ½ cantaloupe melon, cut into chunks
- 1 cup (240ml) fresh orange juice
- 1 banana, peeled and cut into chunks
- ½ cup (120ml) fig juice
- 1 fresh fig, sliced, for garnish

METHOD

1. Blend the ingredients together until smooth.
2. Pour into glasses, and garnish with the fig slices.

Blackberry Pie

This is the rare drink that works well cold or warm. Try it warm with your favorite alcohol-free spirit for perfect autumn morning relaxation.

INGREDIENTS

- 2 handfuls blackberries
- 1 cup (240ml) apple juice
- 1 pinch ground cinnamon
- Cinnamon stick, for garnish

METHOD

1. Blend the blackberries and apple juice together.
2. Stir in the cinnamon. Serve cool or warm it over a moderate heat and garnish with a cinnamon stick.

Tropical Iced Tea

This sweet iced tea has a bit of a bite thanks to the tartness in the lemon juice. It's the perfect brew for a hot summer day. Makes enough to mix 3 to 4 drinks.

INGREDIENTS

- ½ cup (45g) fresh pineapple sage leaves, packed
- ½ cup (120ml) pineapple juice, poured into ice-cube trays and frozen
- 1 tsp. (5ml) lemon juice
- 4 cups (960ml) water
- Honey to taste

METHOD

1. Boil the water, add the pineapple sage leaves and lemon juice, and leave to steep for twenty minutes.
2. Strain the leaves, pour into a glass, add honey to taste, and add three to five frozen pineapple-juice cubes.

Pacific Perfection

Enjoy this drink as-is or mix in some soda water or botanicals for a tropical break on a breezy pacific beach.

INGREDIENTS

- 1 cup (240ml) pineapple juice
- ½ mango, peeled and cut into chunks
- Pulp of 2 passion fruit

METHOD

1. Blend the pineapple juice and mango and pour into a glass.
2. Stir in the passion fruit pulp.

Blue Spice

This is another unusually spiced fruit mix that works well on its own but would be a delightful base for cold-weather cocktails.

INGREDIENTS

- 1 cup (240ml) fresh orange juice
- 3 handfuls blueberries
- 1 cup (240ml) apple juice
- 2 pinches ground nutmeg
- 1 pinch ground cinnamon

METHOD

1. Blend the orange juice, blueberries, and apple juice.
2. Pour into a glass and stir in the nutmeg and cinnamon.

Cool Down Cordial

Cordials are traditionally drinks meant to revive, cheer, or invigorate and this fresh blend will hopefully refresh you on days when you need it. This mix would also be fantastic with a bit of lemon juice or an herbal element.

INGREDIENTS

- 1 cup (240ml) apple juice
- 12½ oz. (354g) plums, halved and stoned
- 3½ oz. (100g) blackberries
- Thin strips of apple, for garnish

METHOD

1. Blend the apple juice, plums, and blackberries until smooth.
2. Pour into glasses and garnish with thin strips of apple.

Passion

Passion fruit is growing in popularity. It has a potent, complex flavor so a little bit can go a long way, especially in a light summer beverage.

INGREDIENTS

- 1 banana, cut into chunks
- 1 part fresh orange juice
- 1 part mango juice
- 2 large spoons passion fruit pulp
- Ice cubes
- Maraschino cherry, for garnish

METHOD

1. Blend all ingredients for about 10 seconds.
2. Fill a tall glass with ice cubes and pour the fruit juice mix over it. Garnish with a cherry on a stick.

Passionate Peach

This is a perfect drink for brunches. Serve unmixed or add sparkling white grape juice to an out-of-the-ordinary alcohol-free mimosa.

INGREDIENTS

- 2 peaches, halved and stoned
- 8 fresh mint leaves, chopped
- Pulp of 2 passion fruits
- 4 ice cubes
- 1 sprig fresh mint, for garnish

METHOD

1. Blend the peaches and mint together.
2. Stir in the passion fruit pulp and pour over ice. Garnish with a sprig of mint.

Golden Glow

It's hard to go wrong with a golden sunny beverage mixer.

INGREDIENTS

- 1 part apricot juice
- 1 part mango juice
- 1 part peach juice
- 1 part orange juice
- Orange zest, for garnish

METHOD

1. Combine the juices and pour into glasses.

Calendula Sun Tea

This old-fashioned process for "brewing" tea harkens back to a simpler time. Add a little honey to balance out the sometimes spicy flavor of the calendula flowers. This recipe makes enough to mix 3 to 4 drinks.

INGREDIENTS

- 1 cup (89g) fresh calendula flowers
- 4 cups (960ml) cold water
- Honey to taste

METHOD

1. Fill a 2-quart (1.9-liter) jar with the fresh flowers and cold water and seal with an airtight lid.
2. Choose a sunny day and leave the jar on a windowsill for at least eight hours.
3. Strain the flowers and pour the liquid over ice.

Scarlet Woman

This is a nice refreshing beverage for those who want a savory treat. It would work well as an alcohol-free Bloody Mary alternative.

INGREDIENTS

- 8 oz. (227g) ripe tomatoes, quartered
- 8 large fresh basil leaves
- 3 spring onions, trimmed
- 1 red pepper, halved and deseeded
- Salt and black pepper to taste
- Crushed ice to serve
- Fresh basil leaves to garnish

METHOD

1. Place the tomatoes, basil leaves, onions, and pepper in the blender and blend until smooth.
2. Pour into a glass over ice, add seasoning to taste, and garnish with basil leaves.

Raspberry Zinger

This is a mixer with some serious flavors: tart raspberry, sharp lime, sweet orange juice, and a final, energizing zap of mint.

INGREDIENTS

- 3 large scoops raspberries
- 1 cup (240ml) lime juice
- 1 cup (240ml) fresh orange juice
- 6 fresh mint leaves, finely chopped
- 3 ice cubes

METHOD

1. Blend the raspberries, lime juice, and orange juice together.
2. Stir in the mint leaves and pour over ice cubes.

Chamomile Calm

Cool iced tea is a perfect mixer for hot days. Chamomile helps make this a great relaxing beverage and the papaya adds sweet creaminess.

INGREDIENTS

- 7 fl. oz. (210ml) cold chamomile tea, made with 2 tea bags
- 1 papaya, peeled, halved, and deseeded
- Ice cubes to serve

METHOD

1. Put the chamomile tea and papaya in the blender and blend until smooth.
2. Pour into a glass over ice.

Peppermint Raspberry Tea

The sweetness of the raspberries balances the cool "bite" of the peppermint in this refreshing tea. Over ice, peppermint raspberry tea is a great thirst quencher, but the minty tea with a hint of sweetness can also be enjoyed hot. This recipe makes enough to mix 3 to 4 drinks.

INGREDIENTS

- 1 large scoop fresh peppermint leaves
- 1 large scoop fresh raspberries
- 4 cups (960ml) water

METHOD

1. Bring a kettle of water to a boil.
2. Pour the boiling water over the peppermint leaves and raspberries and leave the brew to steep overnight.
3. To drink, strain the leaves and berries and reheat, or pour the tea over a cup of ice.

Mmm Mint Iced Tea

Hot or iced, mint tea is nice, and these three mint varieties, each with their own distinct flavor, blend perfectly in a tangy but not-too-sweet cup of tea. You can also enjoy this tea hot by allowing the ingredients to steep for only ten minutes and straining into a warm mug. Makes enough to mix 3 to 4 drinks.

INGREDIENTS

- 1 tsp. (1.1g) fresh spearmint leaves
- 1 tsp. (1.1g) fresh peppermint leaves
- 1 tsp. (1.1g) fresh lavender mint leaves
- 4 cups (960ml) water

METHOD

1. Boil the water, add the leaves, and allow to steep in the refrigerator overnight.
2. Strain the leaves, pour the water over ice, and sip.

Carrot and Mango Crush

This bright orange mixer is a healthy and delicious and you can easily use it to create unusual and surprising drinks.

INGREDIENTS

- 3½ fl. oz. (105ml) fresh orange juice
- Flesh of 1 mango, cut into chunks
- 3 oz. (75g) carrots, trimmed and chopped
- Crushed ice, for serving
- Extra mango slice, for garnish

METHOD

1. Place the orange juice and mango in the blender and blend, then add the carrots and blend until smooth.
2. Pour into a glass over crushed ice and garnish with the mango slice.

Citrus City

There are few more enjoyable ways to get our daily dose of vitamin C than mixing a beautiful, refreshing drink.

INGREDIENTS

- 1 part grapefruit juice
- 1 part fresh orange juice
- Juice of ½ lemon
- Juice of ½ lime

METHOD

1. Combine the juices together and stir.

Refreshing Hibiscus Tea

Hibiscus is a tropical flower with a tart, refreshing flavor. Pour it over ice and imagine sipping it on the beach—or brew a cup as a pick-me-up after a day of working in the garden. Makes enough to mix 6 to 8 drinks.

INGREDIENTS

- 1½ cups (135g) dried hibiscus flowers
- 1 cup (200g) sugar
- 2 tsp. (12g) grated ginger
- 1 squirt lime juice
- 8 cups (1.9L) water, separated
- Ice, for serving

METHOD

1. Boil 4 cups (960ml) of water.
2. Add the hibiscus flowers and ginger to the boiling water and let rest for one hour.
3. Strain the flowers and then add the sugar, remaining 4 cups (960ml) of water, and a squirt of lime juice.
4. Stir and serve over ice.

Beet Bliss

If you're craving an unexpected drink, this mix is the one for you: sweet, earthy, and tangy all at the same time.

INGREDIENTS

- 4½ oz. (125g) cooked beets, cut into chunks
- 4½ oz. (125g) yogurt
- 1 clove garlic, peeled and chopped
- ½ oz. (10g) fresh chives, chopped
- 3½ fl. oz. (105ml) apple juice
- Extra fresh chives, for garnish

METHOD

1. Place all the ingredients in a blender and blend until smooth.
2. Pour into a glass and garnish with chives.

Creamy Crimson

This is another one of those unusual savory blends that will work well as a base for brunch cocktails and weekend mixes.

INGREDIENTS

- 2 cups (480ml) beet juice
- 3½ fl. oz. (105ml) yogurt
- 1 tsp. (6g) mustard seeds, plus an extra pinch for sprinkling

METHOD

1. Blend the beet juice with the remaining ingredients until smooth.
2. Serve with a sprinkling of mustard seeds on top.

Bright Eyes

One easy way to create a unique drink base is to try blending sweet fruit with the fresh flavors of vegetables and herbs.

INGREDIENTS

- 2 cups (480ml) carrot juice
- 1 cup (240ml) apple juice
- 2 cups (480ml) fresh orange juice
- 2 Tbsp. (15g) fresh parsley, chopped

METHOD

1. Combine the juices and pour into glasses.
2. Sprinkle the parsley on top.

Carrot Charger

Spirulina is a type of blue-green algae that is high in antioxidants, making it a popular ingredient with many health-conscious people. The savory, salty flavor is similar to seaweed and can be an acquired taste. Adding it in small amounts to a strong mix of carrot and orange juices creates an unusual mix that's energizing and refreshing.

INGREDIENTS

- 1 cup (240ml) carrot juice
- 1 cup (240ml) fresh orange juice
- 2 tsp. (10g) spirulina powder
- 1 tsp. (5g) sesame seeds

METHOD

1. Mix the juices together.
2. Stir in the spirulina and sesame seeds.

CHAPTER 4:
After Dinner Drinks

Drinking coffee or tea after dinner is a tradition for many around the world. Caffeine can help combat the lethargy you might feel after enjoying a satisfying meal and coffees and teas can aid or kick-start digestion, help us relax, and even soothe headaches. Much like the drinks in the previous chapter, these delicious brews can also serve as base mixers for your own cocktail experimentation. Splash in some alcohol-free spirits or flavorful syrups to create something that's truly unique.

Try this uplifting Lemon Balm Blend. Recipe on page 174.

Cold Brew Coffee

Cold brew coffee has increased in popularity because of its sweet and rich flavor. The cold-water brewing method retains body and the natural oils in coffee. The acidity is lessened, while the coffee flavor is left intact.

INGREDIENTS

- 1 oz. (28g) coarse ground coffee
- 4¾ cups (1.1L) filtered water
- More water or cream, to taste

METHOD

1. Pour filtered water into your cold brew coffee maker's pitcher.
2. Pour the coffee grounds into the infuser and insert it into the pitcher.
3. Steep for 12 to 24 hours and dilute with water or add a splash of cream to taste.

Thai Iced Coffee

This is a concoction of spices and coffee that complement each other perfectly. The cardamom spice kicks it up a bit and leaves a pleasant aftertaste.

INGREDIENTS

- 6 Tbsp. (108g) freshly fine-ground specialty coffee
- ¼ tsp. (1.5g) ground coriander powder
- 4 or 5 whole green cardamom pods, ground
- Simple syrup, to taste
- 8 ice cubes
- 1 fl. oz. (30ml) heavy whipped cream

METHOD

1. Place the coffee and spices in the filter cone of the brewer. Brew coffee as usual and allow to cool.
2. Add simple syrup to a tall glass. Add 8 ice cubes and pour coffee up to 1 in. (2.5cm) from the top of the glass.
3. Hold the back of a spoon over the glass and slowly pour the heavy whipped cream over the spoon onto the coffee, creating a layered look. This will prevent the cream from dispersing into the coffee right away.
4. Serve with a flexible straw and a tall spoon.

Iced Coffee Americano

An Americano lets you enjoy the full flavor of espresso without the intensity. It is usually brewed fresh for each person and can be adjusted to taste by adding or removing espresso. The Iced Coffee Americano is the chilled version using coffee ice cubes, see page 25.

INGREDIENTS

- Coffee ice cubes
- 10 fl. oz. (300ml) filtered water
- 2 espressos
- Simple syrup, optional

METHOD

1. Fill a tall glass with coffee ice cubes and pour in the chilled filtered ice water.
2. Add the espresso and stir.
3. Stir in simple syrup, to taste.

Summer Sun

A sweet summertime treat created by barista Stefanie Raymond of Barista Daily Grind, Kearny, Nebraska, USA, as an alternative to regular iced coffee. This mix can be shaken and poured into freezer-cold glasses for a frosty effect.

INGREDIENTS

- 1 fl. oz. (30ml) espresso or cold brew coffee
- ½ fl. oz. (15ml) butterscotch
- 1 tsp. (5ml) honey
- ½ fl. oz. (15ml) caramel
- Honey stick straws, for serving

METHOD

1. Mix all ingredients together.
2. Pour into chilled long glasses and serve with honey stick straws.

Espresso Spritz

The simplest sparkling espresso drink ever! It's fresh and easy!

INGREDIENTS

- 1 espresso
- 2 fl. oz. (60ml) sparkling water
- A few ice cubes
- 1 lemon wedge

METHOD

1. Add the espresso to the sparkling water, then add ice and gently stir.
2. Rub the rim of the glass with a lemon wedge, then place the wedge on the rim.

Vietnamese Iced Coffee

After a spicy meal of Vietnamese food, this cool creamy coffee is just what's needed. It is sweet and freshly made each time, using a special Vietnamese coffee press. If you can't find a Vietnamese coffee press, regular strength espresso is an adequate substitute. Enjoy warm or try it over ice.

INGREDIENTS

- 2 to 4 Tbsp. (36 to 72g) finely ground dark roast coffee
- 2 to 4 Tbsp. (30 to 60ml) sweetened condensed milk
- 2 cups (480ml) boiling water
- 1 glass coffee ice cubes

METHOD

1. Place ground coffee in Vietnamese coffee press and screw down the lid.

2. Put the sweetened condensed milk in the bottom of a coffee cup and set the coffee maker on the rim.
3. Pour boiling water over the screw lid of the press.
4. Adjust the tension on the screw lid until bubbles appear throughout the water, and the coffee drips slowly out the bottom of the press.
5. When all water has dripped through, stir the milk and coffee together. If drinking cold, pour over the coffee ice cubes.

Naked Verbena

Refreshing as it is unique, this drink was conjured up by Heather Perry, 2003 Western Regional Barista Champion and 2003 US Barista Champion, of Coffee Klatch, San Dimas, California, USA. She was inspired while living in southern California where verbena plants sometimes grow wild.

INGREDIENTS

- 6 scoops of ice cubes
- ¼ lemon wedge
- 12 lemon verbena leaves
- 4 fl. oz. (120ml) simple syrup, divided into 4
- 8 shots espresso or 8 fl. oz. (240ml) cold brew coffee
- The peel of one lemon, divided into 4

METHOD

1. Combine four scoops of ice cubes with the quartered lemon wedges and eight lemon verbena leaves.
2. Squeeze the juice of the lemons onto the verbena leaves and then freeze the ice mixture.
3. Once the ice mixture is frozen, divide it between four martini glasses.
4. Pour simple syrup onto the ice in each glass.
5. Prepare fresh shots of espresso and pour into a cocktail shaker with the lemon rind and the remaining four lemon verbena leaves. Add the remaining two scoops of ice and shake vigorously.
6. Pour evenly into the four glasses and garnish with a curled lemon peel.

Iced Mint Java

Coffee ice cubes maintain the coffee flavor while the mint leaf adds an aromatic flair.

INGREDIENTS

- Coffee ice cubes
- Chilled double-strength coffee
- Mint syrup
- A small amount of chilled whipped cream
- A sprig of fresh mint leaves

METHOD

1. Fill a tall glass with coffee ice cubes and cover with chilled coffee.
2. Add a dash of mint syrup and stir well.
3. Top with a dollop of chilled, whipped cream to taste, and garnish with a fresh mint sprig.

Shakerato

This classic coffee cocktail from Fritz Storm, World Champion Barista 2002, of Denmark, can be whipped up in seconds. Friends and family will enjoy watching you prepare it. To mix multiple drinks, increase the shaker size and multiply the ingredients by the number of servings.

INGREDIENTS

- 1 fl. oz. (30ml) espresso or coffee of choice
- 1 Tbsp. (15ml) liquid sugar
- 6 ice cubes

METHOD

1. Put all the ingredients in a cocktail shaker and shake rapidly for 45 seconds.
2. Serve in a chilled champagne glass and garnish with a decorative stir stick.

Iced Flavored Coffee Martini

Espresso, double-strength coffee, or cold brew coffee can be used to prepare this elegant signature drink.

INGREDIENTS

- 1 fl. oz. (30ml) almond or hazelnut syrup
- 2 cups (480ml) double-strength brewed coffee
- ½ cup (120ml) fresh cold milk
- Coffee ice cubes
- Chocolate-covered coffee beans or a mint sprig and decorative straws, for garnish

METHOD

1. Pour a small amount of flavored syrup into a cocktail shaker.
2. Add the coffee and fresh cold milk.
3. Fill the shaker with coffee ice cubes and shake vigorously.
4. Pour into martini glasses and add a straw. Garnish with chocolate-covered coffee beans or a mint sprig.

Black Forest

The flavors of chocolate, grenadine, coffee, and cream make for a beautiful drink that tastes like its dessert namesake.

INGREDIENTS

- 1 fl. oz. (30ml) chocolate syrup
- 1 fl. oz. (30ml) toasted marshmallow syrup or whipped cream
- ½ fl. oz. (15ml) grenadine
- 6 fl. oz. (180ml) cold brew coffee
- Grated chocolate, for garnish

METHOD

1. Mix the syrups and grenadine together in a martini glass and add the cold brew coffee.
2. Gently spoon the whipped cream onto the drink.
3. Spiral a toothpick through the drink to make patterns, wiping the toothpick each time to ensure a distinct design.
4. Sprinkle with grated chocolate.

Budding Rose

This drink from Coffee People in Portland, Oregon, USA, can be made with any reddish fruit-flavored syrup. It's an attractive drink, and the colors of the milk, red syrup, and espresso will marble slightly.

INGREDIENTS

- 2 fl. oz. (60ml) alcohol-free tequila
- 10 fl. oz. (300ml) milk or cream
- 3 fl. oz. (90ml) strawberry, cherry, blackberry, or raspberry syrup
- Ice cubes
- 1 fl. oz. (30ml) espresso or cold brew coffee

METHOD

1. Pour alcohol-free tequila, milk or cream, and fruit syrup over ice cubes into a chilled tall glass or pint glass.
2. Add the espresso or cold brew coffee and serve chilled, iced, or at room temperature.

Caffè Calabrese

The orange-infused caramel and melted chocolate discs are just two of the many layers in this winning signature drink created by Sammy Piccolo, 2003 and 2004 Canadian Barista Champion and 2004 World Latte Art Champion, Artigiano, Vancouver, BC, Canada.

INGREDIENTS

- 1 fl. oz. (30ml) orange-infused caramel
- 2 fl. oz. (60ml) toasted almond Chantilly cream
- 1 chocolate disc, preferably 70% dark chocolate
- ¾ fl. oz. (22ml) filtered water added to ½ fl. oz. (15ml) ristretto espresso

METHOD

1. Pour orange-infused caramel in a martini glass, then slowly pour in toasted almond Chantilly cream to create two layers.
2. Place chocolate disc on top and slowly pour water and espresso mixture on top of the chocolate disc.

The White-Cin

This beautiful combination of white chocolate sauce and cinnamon was created by Joe Hayek, 2002 Lebanese Barista Champion, Casper and Gambini's, Beirut, Lebanon.

INGREDIENTS

- 1 fl. oz. (30ml) espresso
- 1 fl. oz. (30ml) cold milk
- 4 fl. oz. (120ml) white chocolate sauce
- 6 ice cubes
- Cinnamon powder
- Small amount of white chocolate shavings
- Cinnamon stick

METHOD

1. Place espresso, cold milk, and white chocolate sauce into a cocktail shaker with the ice cubes and shake for 45 seconds.
2. Pour into chilled wine glasses and top with a layer of cinnamon powder and white chocolate shavings.
3. Garnish with a cinnamon stick.

Cappucine

This is a sophisticated drink that's ideal for after dinner, with a mint cream chocolate on the side.

INGREDIENTS

- 4 parts light cream
- 1 part peppermint cordial or syrup
- Crushed ice
- Grated dark chocolate, for garnish

METHOD

1. Place the cream and peppermint cordial in a cocktail shaker with a scoop of crushed ice.
2. Shake well and strain into a wine glass.
3. Sprinkle a little grated dark chocolate over the top.

Viennese Coffee

Soft cream greets your lips as the orange essence tickles your nose. Wintertime coffees are a welcomed reward for guests who've braved the cold for a visit.

INGREDIENTS

- 4 oz. (113g) semi-sweet or dark chocolate
- 1 tsp. (6g) sugar
- ½ cup (120ml) whipping cream
- 4 cups (960ml) hot strong coffee
- Whipped cream and orange rind, for garnish

METHOD

1. Melt chocolate in a heavy saucepan over low heat and stir in sugar and whipping cream.
2. Blend coffee with a wire whisk, ½ cup (120ml) at a time, until creamy.
3. Top with a dollop of whipped cream and grated orange rind.

Dutch Coffee

Something about a buttery cinnamon stick floating in coffee makes this drink feel like a special occasion beverage.

INGREDIENTS

- 1 cup (240ml) strong brewed coffee
- ½ cup (120ml) cream
- Cinnamon stick
- Small pat of butter

METHOD

1. Blend the coffee and cream in a saucepan and pour the mixture into a mug.
2. Take the cinnamon stick and dip it in the butter.
3. Lay the cinnamon stick flat across the coffee surface and the rim of the mug. The cinnamon stick will float as the butter melts.

Emerald Coffee Cooler

The Emerald Coffee Cooler by Mark Pfaff, Jasper's Coffee House, Federal Way, WA, USA, creatively combines ingredients that might not normally meet in a glass. This recipe makes four drinks.

INGREDIENTS

- 8 fl. oz. (240ml) heavy whipping cream
- 4 tsp. (24g) sugar
- ½ cup (120ml) jellied mint leaves
- 2 tsp. (10ml) caramel sauce
- 2 tsp. (10ml) cinnamon syrup
- 4 fl. oz. (120ml) espresso
- Mint leaves and 1 strawberry, for garnish

METHOD

1. Whip the cream and sugar in a blender until thickened but pourable.
2. Thin the jellied mint leaves in a blender and fold them into the cream.
3. Pour the mint cream into four pint glasses and chill.
4. Dissolve the caramel sauce and syrup into the espresso.
5. Insert a small funnel through the chilled cream mixture to the bottom of the glass and slowly pour the espresso mixture into the funnel while lifting it. The warm liquid will stay in the bottom of the cup as the chilled mint cream mixture rises, creating two distinct layers and colors.
6. Garnish the drink with mint leaves and a sliced strawberry if desired.

Layered Caffé Latte

Espresso and milk offer not only a flavorful treat but also a visual treat. The brown ring of espresso swirls and waves in the milky white layers until a spoon interrupts the bands of color.

INGREDIENTS

- 8 fl. oz. (240ml) milk
- 1 espresso

METHOD

1. Steam the milk to 150° F (65.5° C) and allow to rest. Pour the freshly prepared espresso into a small preheated pitcher.
2. Add the steamed milk to a tall glass, using a spoon to hold back the foam while pouring, then top the milk with a small amount of the foam to the rim of the glass.
3. Gently pour the espresso into the glass. The espresso will pour through the foam and settle on top of the milk, creating a nice layered effect.

Amoré

A simple and elegant drink to serve in fluted glasses or wide-brimmed stem glasses with a touch of added romance and sweetness from the chocolate-dipped strawberry garnish.

INGREDIENTS

- 1 cup (240ml) hot brewed coffee or espresso
- 1 Tbsp. (15ml) strawberry syrup
- 1 chocolate-dipped strawberry, for garnish

METHOD

1. Pour hot coffee into glass, then gently stir in the strawberry syrup.
2. Slice the chocolate-dipped strawberry and place on the rim.

Honeysweet Coffee

Most cocktails are designed to be enjoyed at sunset or later. This one can be enjoyed at any time—even breakfast.

INGREDIENTS

- 1 tsp. (5ml) runny honey
- 1 mug of hot strong black coffee
- 5 ice cubes
- 1 dash aromatic bitters
- Whipped cream and grated nutmeg, for garnish

METHOD

1. Dissolve the honey in the mug of hot coffee and allow to cool.
2. When ready to serve, place five ice cubes in a cocktail shaker, add the dash of bitters, pour in the cold coffee mixture, and shake well.
3. Strain into a tall glass, add a dollop of whipped cream, and dust with grated nutmeg.

Coconut Zesta

This uniquely balanced combination of flavors from Phuong Tran, second place 2004 USBC, first place Northwest Barista Jam, Lava Java Café, Ridgefield, WA, USA, is creamy, comforting, and energizing all at the same time.

INGREDIENTS

- 6 fl. oz. (180ml) coconut milk
- 6 fl. oz. (180ml) milk
- 2 Tbsp. (36g) raw sugar, plus more for dusting the cup rim
- 1 espresso
- Zest of 1 lime
- 2 lime leaves

METHOD

1. Combine the milks and steam or heat the mix in a saucepan.
2. Dust the rim of a preheated cappuccino cup with raw sugar, then brew the espresso directly into the cup.
3. Add raw sugar into the espresso and stir until it dissolves.
4. Pour the steamed or heated milk into the espresso and top it with lime zest.
5. Snap the lime leaves to release aromatics and serve beside the drink on a saucer.

The Blueberry

This drink has a unique flavor with a delightful finish. Kyle Larson, 2004 Northwest Regional Champion, Zoka Coffee Company, Seattle, WA USA, created this elegant drink that is also delicious and unexpected.

INGREDIENTS

- ½ tsp. (2.6g) cinnamon
- 1 Tbsp. (15ml) honey
- 6 espressos
- ½ cup (120ml) heavy whipped cream
- 1 cup (148g) frozen blueberries
- 1 bar dark chocolate, grated cinnamon, and 1 whole cinnamon stick, for garnish

METHOD

1. Add the cinnamon and honey to a cocktail shaker, add the espresso and gently stir with a long whisk to combine it with the cinnamon and honey.
2. Divide the heavy whipped cream into four 2 oz. (60ml) glasses, filling them all halfway.
3. Add frozen blueberries to the cocktail shaker and shake seven times.
4. Pour the espresso mixture over the cream, filling each glass ¾ full.
5. Garnish with dark chocolate, grated cinnamon, and a cinnamon stick.

Mocha After Eight

This beverage can be served up in a designer mug or layered for visual effect in a tall clear glass.

INGREDIENTS

- 1 fl. oz. (30ml) fresh espresso
- 1 fl. oz. (30ml) mint syrup
- 1 Tbsp. (18g) cocoa powder, plus more for garnish
- 1 cup (240ml) steamed milk
- Fresh mint leaf, for garnish

METHOD

1. Blend coffee, syrup, and cocoa powder in preheated cups.
2. Add the steamed milk.
3. Garnish with cocoa powder and a fresh mint leaf.

Mexican Mocha

This traditional blend of chocolate and spices has the added kick of strong coffee flavor.

INGREDIENTS

- 2 fl. oz. (60ml) milk
- 2 cups (480ml) hot double-strength brewed coffee or espresso
- 1 Tbsp. (15ml) chocolate syrup
- 1 pinch each cinnamon and cloves
- 1 chocolate-dipped cinnamon stick, for garnish

METHOD

1. Heat the milk, coffee, chocolate syrup, and spices together on the stove.
2. Pour into a mug and garnish with the chocolate-dipped cinnamon stick.

Caffé Napoli

Small and delicious, this drink from Kyle Larson, 2004 Northwest Regional Barista Champion, Zoka Coffee Company, Seattle, Washington, USA, can be enjoyed after a meal or by the fireside—giving you a sweet treat and coffee all in one sip!

INGREDIENTS

- ¼ cup (60ml) sweetened condensed milk
- 1½ Tbsp. (17.5ml) toasted hazelnut oil
- 1 dash fresh cinnamon
- 1 dash freshly ground cardamom
- 12 fl. oz. (360ml) whole milk
- 4 fl. oz. (120ml) fresh espresso or double-strength coffee
- 1 bar dark chocolate

METHOD

1. Combine the sweetened condensed milk, hazelnut oil, cinnamon, and cardamom in a small mixing bowl and whisk. Place the bowl in hot water to keep it warm.
2. Heat the milk on the stove top (without scalding), set it aside for a while, then whisk.
3. Prepare four shots of espresso or double-strength coffee, pouring each into a 1½ fl. oz. (45ml) demitasse.
4. Add the sweetened condensed milk blend to each demitasse, followed by the whisked steamed milk.
5. Garnish with the dark chocolate.

Monk's Cappuccino

Warming brandy extract livens up this coffee classic without adding alcohol. It can be made with espresso or hot, concentrated coffee.

INGREDIENTS

- 2 fl. oz. (60ml) espresso or hot, concentrated coffee
- ⅔ cup (160ml) hot milk
- 1 Tbsp. (15ml) brandy extract
- 1 tsp. (4g) sugar
- 2 Tbsp. (30ml) white chocolate syrup
- Whipped cream and chocolate shavings, for garnish

METHOD

1. Place all the ingredients in a blender and blend until smooth.
2. Pour the drink into a glass and garnish with whipped cream and chocolate shavings.

Marochino

This is a medium-temperature drink meant to be enjoyed in one sip. The bittersweet chocolate stands up to the intensity of espresso. Fritz Storm, 2002 World Barista Champion, Denmark, created this shot-style drink.

INGREDIENTS

- 1 tsp. (5ml) bitter chocolate sauce
- 2 espressos
- 1 cup (240ml) steamed milk

METHOD

1. Place the chocolate sauce in small glass and add the espresso.
2. Pour in the steamed milk, trying to make some latte art on the top.

Turkish-Style Coffee

Türk Kahvesi is commonly consumed on every street corner in Istanbul. With this improvised recipe you can enjoy the flavors of Turkey without leaving your kitchen!

INGREDIENTS

- 1 cup (82g) ground dark roast coffee
- 1 Tbsp. (18g) ground cardamom
- 8 cups (1.9L) water
- ¾ cup (150g) sugar
- Whole cardamom pods, for garnish

METHOD

1. Combine coffee and cardamom in a brewer filter basket and brew coffee as usual.
2. Whisk in the sugar.
3. Serve in a small, preheated demitasse and float whole cardamom pods on top for a nice visual effect.

The Marquis

Several spices are combined here to create a complex drink that has style, class, and balance. This perfect rainy-day pick-me-up was created by US Barista Championship judge Alexarc Mastema, Black Drop Coffeehouse, Bellingham, Washington, USA.

INGREDIENTS

- ¼ fl. oz. (7ml) cinnamon syrup
- ½ fl. oz. (15ml) vanilla syrup
- 1 fl. oz. (30ml) espresso or strong brewed coffee
- 1 pinch ground chicory
- 1 pinch ground cinnamon
- 1 pinch brown sugar
- ½ cup (120ml) milk

METHOD

1. Mix cinnamon and vanilla syrup in a cup.
2. Brew the espresso or coffee with chicory, then pour in the syrups and mix well.
3. Add cinnamon and brown sugar and allow it to melt undisturbed.
4. Steam or heat the milk on the stove and stir so that it does not burn, then slowly pour over the coffee, syrup, and spice mix to make latte art.

Cilantro Mint Tea

These bright, citrus flavors come together to create a refreshing cup of tea. Because both herbs are known to aid digestion, cilantro mint tea is a great choice for an after-dinner brew.

INGREDIENTS

- 1 Tbsp. (1g) fresh cilantro leaves, packed
- 1 Tbsp. (1.8g) fresh peppermint leaves
- 2 tsp. (4g) orange peel, coarsely chopped
- 1 tsp. (2g) fresh ginger, finely chopped
- 2 cups (480ml) water
- Honey to taste

METHOD

1. Place the herbs, orange peel, and ginger in a cup. Gently crush with the back of a small spoon to release the essential oils.
2. Bring the water to a boil and pour the hot water over the herb mixture and let it steep for five to seven minutes.
3. Strain the leaves and stir in honey to taste.

Ginger Snap Macchiato

This tasty and attractive combination from Teri Bryany, Black Drop Coffee House, Bellingham, WA, USA, melds nicely as a designer drink. It has style, taste, and texture.

INGREDIENTS

- ½ Tbsp (7.5ml) molasses
- ¼ tsp. (1.5ml) caramel
- 1 pinch ground ginger
- 1 fl. oz. (30ml) espresso
- 1 pinch ground cinnamon
- ½ cup (120ml) steamed milk

METHOD

1. Add molasses and caramel into a wide-rim demitasse and sprinkle with ground ginger.
2. Add the espresso slowly to preserve the crema on top, then sprinkle with the ground cinnamon.
3. Carefully pour the steamed milk over the espresso, creating latte art.

Sleepytime Tea

The subtly sweet flavors and heady scents of the herbs in this best-before-bed brew can help you drift into dreamland.

INGREDIENTS

- 1 Tbsp. (5g) dried lemon balm
- 1 Tbsp. (5g) dried peppermint
- 1 Tbsp. (5g) dried rose petals
- 1 Tbsp. (5g) dried lavender leaves
- 1 tsp. (2g) fennel seeds
- 4 cups (960ml) water
- Honey to taste

METHOD

1. Bring the water to a boil and then add the lemon balm, peppermint, rose petals, lavender leaves, and fennel seeds. Let the tea steep for five minutes.
2. Strain the herbs, pour the tea into a warm mug, add honey to taste, and sip.

Hot Orange Spiced Tea

This evening warmer is perfect for sipping next to a blazing fire while the snow falls outside.

INGREDIENTS

- 1 large lemon
- 1 large orange
- 1½ pt. (700 ml) water
- 4 to 5 cloves
- 1 stick of cinnamon
- 3 green tea bags
- Honey or sugar to taste
- Cinnamon sticks and orange slices, for garnish

METHOD

1. Squeeze the juice from the lemon and the orange.
2. Put the water, cloves, and cinnamon in a saucepan and bring to the boil. Remove from the heat and leave to stand for 1 minute, then add the tea bags.
3. Set aside to infuse for 5 minutes.
4. Remove the tea bags and, if sweetening, stir in honey or sugar to taste. Strain in the lemon and orange juices and reheat gently.
5. Garnish with cinnamon sticks and orange slices.

Lavender Lemon Tea

Although these herbs are opposites when it comes to their effects—lavender is calming and lemon is uplifting—the iconic flavors pair perfectly in a tea that has a sweet floral essence. You can enjoy this drink warm, or, if you'd like to try it iced, allow the ingredients to steep overnight before straining over ice.

INGREDIENTS

- 1 Tbsp. (5g) dried lavender leaves
- 1Tbsp. (5g) dried lemon balm leaves
- 4 cups (960ml) water

METHOD

1. Bring the water to a boil, add the lavender and lemon balm, and steep for five minutes.
2. Strain the herbs, pour into a warm mug, and serve.

Caffé Mocha

For those who like chocolate, the Caffé Mocha is an excellent introduction into the world of espresso coffees. As smooth as rich hot cocoa, with a slight hint of espresso flavor, this drink is perfect for chilly winter mornings or evenings.

INGREDIENTS

- 8 fl. oz. (240ml) milk
- ½ fl. oz. (15ml) chocolate syrup
- 1 espresso
- Chocolate shavings and whipped cream, for garnish

METHOD

1. Steam the milk and set it aside.
2. Place the syrup into a tall glass, then add the espresso and mix thoroughly until the syrup dissolves.
3. Fill the glass with the steamed milk, stir, top with the whipped cream, and dust with chocolate shavings.

Lemon Balm Blend

Lemon is both calming and uplifting, making it a great choice if you're anxious or feeling blue. Before taking your first sip, breathe in the invigorating scent.

INGREDIENTS

- ½ cup (15g) fresh peppermint leaves
- ½ cup (15g) fresh lemon balm leaves
- 2 cups (480ml) water

METHOD

1. Place the peppermint and lemon balm leaves in a teapot.
2. Bring a kettle of water to a boil and pour it over the leaves, leaving it to steep for three to five minutes.
3. Strain the leaves before drinking.

Immune-Boosting Blend

Starting to feel under the weather? The sweet and pungent flavor combination in this healing tea can help. If the ginger is too pungent, cut the quantity or add honey to taste.

INGREDIENTS

- 1 Tbsp. (5g) dried echinacea
- ½ cup (72g) fresh strawberries
- 1 Tbsp. (5g) dried rose hips
- 1 Tbsp. (6g) grated ginger
- 4 cups (960ml) water

METHOD

1. Bring the water to a boil and then add echinacea, strawberries, rose hips, and ginger.
2. Let the tea steep for at least thirty minutes.
3. Strain the herbs, pour into a warm mug, and sip.

Citrus Lift Tea

Need a pick-me-up? The distinct citrus flavors in these popular herbs blend perfectly for an uplifting (and aromatic) cup of tea.

INGREDIENTS

- 1 Tbsp. (1.8g) fresh lemon verbena leaves
- 1 Tbsp. (1.8g) fresh lemon balm leaves
- 1 Tbsp. (1.8g) fresh bee balm leaves
- 4 cups (960ml) water

METHOD

1. Boil the water, add the lemon verbena, lemon balm, and bee balm, and steep for three to five minutes.
2. Strain the leaves, pour the tea into a warm mug, and serve.

Headache Relief Tea

Sipping a cup of Headache Relief Tea and inhaling the aroma of the herbs can help ease a tension headache. The peppermint adds a little tang to the sweet floral flavor, making this a cup of tea you'll want to drink even when you don't have a headache.

INGREDIENTS

- 1 Tbsp. (1.8g) fresh peppermint leaves
- 1 Tbsp. (1.8g) fresh chamomile flowers
- 1 Tbsp. (1.8g) fresh apple mint leaves
- 4 cups (960ml) water

METHOD

1. Boil the water, add the peppermint leaves, chamomile flowers, and apple mint leaves, and steep for three to five minutes.
2. Strain the leaves, pour the tea into a warm mug, and serve.

Weedy Brew

Think twice before ridding the garden of weeds. The earthy flavors of chickweed, dandelion, and red clover—not to mention their healing properties—make a unique savory tea.

INGREDIENTS

- 2 Tbsp. (3.6g) fresh chickweed
- 2 Tbsp. (3.6g) fresh dandelion flowers
- 2 Tbsp. (3.6g) fresh red clover
- 4 cups (960ml) water
- Honey to taste

METHOD

1. Thoroughly wash all the ingredients.
2. Boil the water in a small saucepan, add the chickweed, dandelion flowers, and red clover, and let steep for ten minutes.
3. Strain the leaves and flowers and pour into a warm mug. Add honey to taste.

Night Cap

This sweet, warm apple-citrus beverage will help ease you towards a restful sleep.

INGREDIENTS

- 2 cups (480ml) apple juice
- Juice of 1 lemon
- Juice of 1 orange
- Small piece of cinnamon stick
- Hot water
- 1 to 2 tsp. (5 to 10ml) clear honey, or to taste
- Orange wedges and apple slices to garnish

METHOD

1. Combine the fruit juices and chill.
2. When ready to serve, half fill a glass or mug with the juice mix, add a small piece of cinnamon stick and top up with hot water.
3. Stir in the clear honey to taste and garnish with orange wedges and apple slices. Remove the cinnamon stick before drinking.

Tummy Troubles Tea

Not feeling well? The ingredients in Tummy Troubles Tea have been shown to ease digestive upset, and, thanks to the hint of sweetness in the herbs, the tea will go down like a spoonful of sugar.

INGREDIENTS

- 1 Tbsp. (5g) dried echinacea flowers
- 1 Tbsp. (1.8g) fresh bee balm leaves
- 1 Tbsp. (1.8g) fresh anise hyssop leaves
- 1 Tbsp. (5g) fennel
- 4 cups (960ml) water

METHOD

1. Boil the water and then add the echinacea flowers, bee balm leaves, anise hyssop leaves, and fennel. Steep for three to five minutes.
2. Strain the leaves, pour the tea into a warm mug, and serve.

Winter Warmer

Star anise has a mild and fragrant licorice flavor that adds warmth to this light juice blend.

INGREDIENTS

- 2 parts pear juice
- 1 part apple juice
- 2 star anise pods

METHOD

1. Combine the juices in a saucepan.
2. Add the star anise and slowly bring to a boil and allow to infuse.
3. Pour into a glass and serve warm.

CHAPTER 5:
Dessert Drinks

Everybody loves a good dessert, and these delicious mixed drinks are sweet treats you can enjoy any time. From soda fountain classics like floats, malts, and milkshakes to breakfast-ready fruit smoothies and creamy ice cream coffee blends, you can indulge your sweet tooth all day every day! Some of these desserts will also work well combined with alcohol-free spirits and botanicals, so once you've discovered your favorites, try adding in new elements and see what you create.

Try this delightful Caribbean Dream. Recipe on page 182.

Cranberry Craving

This is a tart citrus smoothie to brighten up fall mornings.

INGREDIENTS

- 5 fl. oz. (150ml) fresh orange juice
- 4½ oz. (127g) yogurt
- 4 oz. (113g) cranberries
- 5 oz. (142g) raspberries
- Ice cubes, for serving
- Fresh mint leaves, for garnish

METHOD

1. Place the orange juice and yogurt into the blender, then add the berries and blend until smooth.
2. Pour into a glass over ice and garnish.

Papaya Passion

Fresh ginger brings an unexpected bit of bite and heat to this creamy sweet dessert drink.

INGREDIENTS

- 4½ oz. (127g) yogurt
- 1 papaya, peeled and deseeded
- ½ medium pineapple, peeled and cut into chunks
- ½ in. (1.3cm) piece fresh ginger, peeled and chopped
- Ice cubes, for serving

METHOD

1. Put the yogurt into the blender first, then add the papaya, pineapple, and ginger. Blend until smooth.
2. Pour into a glass over ice.

Mango Lassi

This favorite Indian beverage is essentially a yogurt-based spiced mango smoothie, and it's easy to make at home!

INGREDIENTS

- 3½ fl. oz. (105ml) still mineral water, chilled
- 1 mango, flesh only
- 4 oz. (113g) yogurt
- 1 pinch cinnamon
- Sliced mango and cinnamon stick, for garnish

METHOD

1. Place the ingredients in the blender and blend until smooth.
2. Pour into a glass and garnish with sliced mango and a cinnamon stick.

Jewels

Topping this beautiful creamy pink drink with a few pomegranate seeds will give the impression of fine rubies scattered on a velvet cushion.

INGREDIENTS

- 1 pomegranate, halved and deseeded
- 1 passion fruit, halved and pulp scooped out
- 3 Tbsp. (54g) yogurt

METHOD

1. Carefully blend the pomegranate seeds, then strain through a fine mesh strainer.
2. Stir in passion-fruit pulp and yogurt, then top with a few whole pomegranate seeds.

Caribbean Dream

This delicious tropical smoothie is the type of drink that will transport you to a summer vacation state of mind.

INGREDIENTS

- 2 bananas, peeled and cut into three or four pieces
- 1 medium mango, peeled and cut into chunks
- 1 medium pineapple, peeled and cut into chunks
- 7 fl. oz. (210ml) coconut milk
- Pineapple wedges and lime slice, for garnish

METHOD

1. Blend the mango and pineapple together then add the banana and coconut milk.
2. Blend until smooth and garnish with a pineapple wedge and lime slice.

Strawberry Orangeana

The combination of strawberry, orange, and banana is a classic mix that creates the perfect smoothie for breakfast or dessert.

INGREDIENTS

- 3 fl. oz. (90ml) fresh orange juice
- 2 oz. (57g) fresh or frozen strawberries
- 1 banana, peeled and cut into chunks
- Ice cubes
- Fresh fruit, for garnish

METHOD

1. Blend the ingredients with ice until smooth and pour into a large parfait glass.
2. Garnish with fresh fruit.

Fruit Smoothie

The easiest way to mix up a fruit smoothie is to pick your favorite fruit juice, add a creamy banana, and blend with your favorite fresh fruit. It's healthy, refreshing dessert alternative.

INGREDIENTS

- 6 fl. oz. (180ml) fresh orange juice
- 1 cup (100–200g) fresh fruit of your choice
- 1 banana
- 1 scoop ice

METHOD

1. Blend all the ingredients until smooth and serve in a tall glass.

Kiwi Kiss

This green smoothie has a light sweetness to it that is balanced nicely with the creaminess of the yogurt and milk and the acidity of the lime juice.

INGREDIENTS

- 2 kiwi fruit, peeled and quartered
- Juice of ½ lime
- 6 oz. (170g) strawberries, hulled
- 4½ oz. (127g) strawberry-flavored yogurt
- 3½ fl. oz. (105ml) milk
- Ice cubes, for serving
- Slice of kiwi fruit, for garnish

METHOD

1. Place the kiwi fruit, lime juice, strawberries, yogurt, and milk in the blender and blend until smooth.
2. Pour into a glass over ice and garnish with a slice of kiwi fruit.

Spiced Banana Smoothie

This drink highlights distinctive saffron, a recognizably red spice derived from saffron crocus flowers. It's long been the world's costliest spice by weight, so this creamy beverage will feel like a deliciously indulgent dessert.

INGREDIENTS

- 1 pinch saffron, soaked in 1 tsp. (5ml) hot water, plus more for garnish
- 1 banana, peeled and cut into chunks
- 4 fl. oz. (120ml) whole milk

METHOD

1. Blend ingredients together, serve in a tall glass, and garnish with a sprinkle of saffron.

Banana Bomb

This delicious drink works as an easy breakfast on busy mornings or as a deliciously creamy afternoon pick-me-up. If including the egg, pregnant women and the elderly should avoid drinking.

INGREDIENTS

- 1 ripe banana, peeled and cut into chunks
- 1 whole egg, optional
- 1 Tbsp. (15ml) runny honey
- Enough chilled whole milk to fill the glass

METHOD

1. Place the banana chunks in a blender.
2. Add the egg, honey, and milk, and blend to a smooth milkshake consistency.
3. Serve in a tall glass.

Wimbledon Winner

Anybody who follows tennis will know that Wimbledon and strawberries and cream are an inseparable match. This drink is the perfect accompaniment to an afternoon watching the finals. You can vary the ingredient quantities to suit your taste.

INGREDIENTS

- 12 fresh strawberries, rinsed and hulled
- Enough single cream to cover the strawberries
- 1 Tbsp. (12.5g) caster sugar
- 1 generous pinch powdered ginger
- Soda water
- Ice cubes

METHOD

1. Place the strawberries, cream, sugar, and ginger in a blender and combine them to a smooth consistency.
2. Pour the blend into a tall glass, add a generous helping of ice cubes then add soda water to almost fill the glass.
3. Stir well before serving.

Fig Fix

This orange fig beverage features soothing vanilla flavors. The discarded vanilla pod can be added to a container filled with sugar to naturally add some vanilla flavor to your baking.

INGREDIENTS

- 1 cup (240ml) fresh orange juice
- 2 fresh figs, stalk removed and halved
- 1 vanilla pod, seeds scooped out
- 6 Tbsp. (100g) yogurt
- 2 tsp. (10ml) honey

METHOD

1. Blend all the ingredients and pour into your favorite glass.

Black Cow

There is nothing as refreshing and delicious as a Black Cow (also known as a Root Beer Float) on a hot summer day. You can also swap the root beer out for cola or any other sweet fizzy soda to create different float colors and flavors.

INGREDIENTS

- 2 scoops vanilla ice cream
- Root beer, well chilled

METHOD

1. Place the ice cream in a tall glass.
2. Pour the root beer over the ice cream and serve with a thick straw and long-handled spoon.

Pink Lassie

This is a delicious dessert beverage that looks sweet and elegant when served up in champagne flutes. It adds a bright touch to any special events.

INGREDIENTS

- 2 fl. oz. (60ml) cranberry juice
- 1 fl. oz. (30ml) pineapple juice
- 1 fl. oz. (30ml) simple syrup
- 1 splash soda water
- 1 scoop vanilla ice cream

METHOD

1. Blend the ingredients until smooth.
2. Serve in a champagne flute.

Toots

This sweet treat plays on the popular chocolate and orange flavor combination. It's a great creamy treat for afternoon picnics.

INGREDIENTS

- 2 fl. oz. (60ml) orange soda
- 1 scoop orange sherbet
- 1 scoop chocolate ice cream
- Whipped cream and 1 orange wedge, for garnish

METHOD

1. Blend the ingredients until smooth and pour into a hurricane glass.
2. Top with the whipped cream and garnish with the orange wedge.

Chocolate Almond Shake

Chocolate and nut flavors are natural companions, hence the large number of chocolate bars that contain nuts. They combine just as well in a drink. This one is particularly rich and decadent and works well as a dessert, especially if you leave out the ice.

INGREDIENTS

- Crushed ice, optional
- 1 part chocolate syrup
- 1 part almond syrup
- 4 parts single cream
- Maraschino cherry, for garnish

METHOD

1. Place a scoop of crushed ice in a cocktail shaker and add the chocolate and almond syrups and the cream.
2. Shake well until smoothly blended, then strain into a wine glass and garnish with a cherry on a stick.

Peach Smoothie

This peach smoothie recipe from Filtron, Huntington Beach, California, USA, is a surprising energizer. Along with the frozen peaches, it features cold brew coffee and coffee ice cubes!

INGREDIENTS

- 1 cup (240ml) cream
- 2 fl. oz. (60ml) cold brew coffee
- 2 Tbsp. (36g) sugar
- 1 large scoop coffee ice cubes
- 1 cup (140g) frozen peaches
- 1 fresh peach slice

METHOD

1. Place all the ingredients in a blender and blend until smooth.
2. Pour into chilled tall glasses.

Frozen Coffee Cooler

This recipe from Sandy Hon of Java Jazz, Kansas City, USA, is incredibly versatile—you can adjust the flavor by trying different syrups either alone or in combination with one another.

INGREDIENTS

- 2 fl. oz. (60ml) vanilla syrup
- 2 fl. oz. (60ml) preferred syrup flavor
- 2 espressos
- 2 fl. oz. (60ml) fresh cream or Chantilly cream
- Crushed or cubed ice

METHOD

1. Blend all ingredients until smooth.
2. Serve either in a martini glass or a tall decorative glass.

Strawberry Milkshake

This is a quick and easy refreshing drink to make in strawberry season. If including the egg, pregnant women and the elderly should avoid drinking.

INGREDIENTS

- 1 scoop of crushed ice
- 1 scoop of fresh strawberries, rinsed and hulled
- 1 cup (240ml) whole milk
- 1 Tbsp. (15ml) runny honey
- 1 whole egg (optional)
- ½ fresh strawberry, for garnish

METHOD

1. Place the crushed ice in a blender and add the strawberries, milk, honey, and egg, if using.
2. Blend until creamy smooth and top with half a strawberry. Serve with a thick straw.

Maple Plum Marvel

This blend of plum, cinnamon, yogurt, and maple combines the perfect flavors of a fruity breakfast pastry into a drink that can be enjoyed throughout the day.

INGREDIENTS

- 1 cup (240ml) plum juice
- 2 pinches ground cinnamon
- 6 Tbsp. (100g) yogurt
- 2 Tbsp. (30ml) maple syrup

METHOD

1. Stir all the ingredients into the plum juice and mix thoroughly.

Lemon Ice Cream Soda

This is a popular summer refresher that's stood the test of time.

INGREDIENTS

- Juice of 1 large lemon
- 2 tsp. (9.3g) caster sugar
- Soda water
- 1 scoop soft vanilla ice cream

METHOD

1. Pour the lemon juice into a tall glass, add the sugar and stir until it has dissolved.
2. Add the soda water to fill the glass to about two-thirds, stir gently, and add a scoop of ice cream.
3. Serve with a thick straw and long-handled spoon.

Orange Cream Fizz

Orange cream popsicles are always an ice cream truck favorite, and this fizzy drink brings that creamy sweet citrus refreshment to your glass. Leave out the soda water and add more ice cream to create a more traditional creamsicle drink.

INGREDIENTS

- 3 fl. oz. (90ml) fresh orange juice
- 3 fl. oz. (90ml) soda water
- 1 scoop vanilla ice cream
- Maraschino cherry, for garnish

METHOD

1. Blend the ingredients until smooth and pour the mixture into a tall glass.
2. Garnish with the cherry.

Lime Freeze

Limes have a sharp citrus flavor that lends itself to summer refreshment. This zingy dessert will wake you up during those long hot days of late summer.

INGREDIENTS

- 3 fl. oz. (90ml) lime juice
- 2 scoops lime sherbet
- 1 lime wedge, for garnish

METHOD

1. Blend the ingredients until smooth.
2. Serve in a large parfait glass and garnish with the lime wedge.

Coffee Milkshake

This smooth coffee milkshake is delicious and easy to prepare. Cup rims can be fancy or plain. Serve with straws on a hot summer day.

INGREDIENTS

- 3 large scoops vanilla ice cream
- 1 cup (240ml) milk
- ½ cup (120ml) chilled cold brew coffee
- 1 tsp. (5ml) vanilla extract
- Whipped cream and chocolate sprinkles, for garnish

METHOD

1. Mix all the ingredients in a blender until smoothly blended.
2. Serve in a tall glass and decorate with whipped cream and chocolate sprinkles.

Coconut Crème Café

Sweet, creamy, and tropical, this dessert coffee from Filtron, Huntington Beach, CA, USA, is designed to satisfy the most nit-picking guests. A welcome refreshment after a spicy meal.

INGREDIENTS

- 1 fl. oz. (30ml) cold brew coffee
- ½ tsp. (2.5ml) alcohol-free coffee liqueur, optional
- 5 fl. oz. (150ml) water
- 2 Tbsp. (30ml) coconut cream
- Whipped cream and coconut flakes, for garnish

METHOD

1. Place all ingredients in a blender and blend for 10 seconds until smooth.
2. Pour the mixture into chilled glasses and garnish with whipped cream and coconut flakes.

Chocolate Fizz

This drink adds a slight sparkle to ordinary chocolate milk. It's also less filling than a milkshake and can work as a dessert or with breakfast.

INGREDIENTS

- 2 Tbsp. (30ml) chocolate syrup, or more to taste
- Cold whole milk
- Soda water

METHOD

1. Pour the chocolate syrup into a tall glass, add the milk to fill about two thirds of the glass, and stir until all the chocolate has dissolved.
2. Top up with soda water and stir gently again before serving.

Rosie's Ruby Heart

I have no idea who Rosie was, but she obviously had a kind heart for somebody to name a drink after her. The freshest fruit always makes the tastiest drinks. **Note:** If you make this with a traditional sour mix (featuring egg white), pregnant women and the elderly should avoid drinking.

INGREDIENTS

- Crushed ice
- 6 fresh strawberries, rinsed and hulled
- 1 cup (240ml) single cream
- 2 Tbsp. (30ml) sour mix, or to taste
- 1 fresh strawberry, for garnish

METHOD

1. Place a scoop of crushed ice in a blender and add the strawberries, cream, and sour mix.
2. Blend until smooth and garnish with the remaining strawberry.

Easter Bunny

This deliciously creamy drink is rich and thick enough to be served as a dessert.

INGREDIENTS

- 3 parts frozen yogurt
- 1 part fresh orange juice
- 1 splash sugar syrup
- Crushed ice
- Slice of peach, for garnish

METHOD

1. Place a scoop of crushed ice and the yogurt, orange juice, and sugar syrup in a blender and blend to a smooth consistency.
2. Pour into a wine goblet and garnish with a slice of ripe peach.

Summer Soda

This is a good drink to enjoy on a hot summer day around the pool. It looks great and tastes even better.

INGREDIENTS

- Juice of 1 orange
- Juice of 1 lemon
- Juice of 1 grapefruit
- Ice cubes
- Soda water
- 1 scoop soft vanilla ice cream
- Glacé cherry, to garnish

METHOD

1. Pour the orange, lemon, and grapefruit juices in a cocktail shaker with five or six ice cubes and shake.
2. Strain into a tall glass, filling it to the halfway mark.
3. Top up to almost full with soda water and add a scoop of vanilla ice cream.
4. Top with a cherry and serve with a straw and long-handled spoon.

Java Chocolate Shake

Ice cream, chocolate, and coffee are always a hit on their own, but Filtron of Huntington Beach, CA, USA, blended them together to get this rich, yummy treat. For a dramatic touch, decorate the interior of the glass with chocolate swirls before adding the shake.

INGREDIENTS

- 1 fl. oz. (30ml) cold brew coffee or espresso
- 3 fl. oz. (90ml) filtered water
- 1 milk chocolate square, roughly chopped
- 2 large scoops vanilla ice cream, softened

METHOD

1. Blend the coffee, filtered water, and chocolate until mixed.
2. Add the softened ice cream and blend until smooth.

Affogato

Served in European cafés and homes alike, no one turns this sweet treat down. It's simple, elegant, and delicious.

INGREDIENTS

- 1 scoop vanilla ice cream
- 1 fl. oz. (30ml) double-strength coffee
- Chocolate-covered coffee beans, optional, for garnish

METHOD

1. Scoop the ice cream into a small, elegant dish or glass.
2. Pour the freshly drawn coffee over the top and garnish with chocolate-covered coffee beans.

Ginger Peach Shake

You can also amp up the dessert style of this drink by reducing the quantity of milk and increasing the ice cream.

INGREDIENTS

- 1 large, fresh peach, peeled and cut into chunks
- Chilled whole milk
- 2 scoops vanilla or peach ice cream
- ¼ tsp. (1.5g) ground ginger
- ¼ tsp. (1.5g) ground cinnamon
- Whipped cream

METHOD

1. Place the peach chunks in a blender, add two tablespoons (30ml) of milk, and blend to a smooth purée.
2. Add the ice cream and about one cup (240ml) of milk, along with the ginger and cinnamon.
3. Blend until smooth, pour into a tall glass, and top with a dollop of whipped cream.
4. Serve with a thick straw.

Chill Out Lemon

This is another cooling citrus beverage to help weather the summer heat. This drink is particularly nice after a long day working in the garden.

INGREDIENTS

- 2 large lemons
- 2 to 3 Tbsp. (28 to 44g) caster sugar, or to taste
- Still mineral or tap water
- 4 large or 8 small scoops of lemon sorbet

METHOD

1. Cut the lemons into chunks and place in a blender with the caster sugar. Blend until smooth.
2. Strain into a measuring cup, pushing as much of the pulp as you can through the strainer with a wooden spoon.
3. Taste the juice and add more sugar to taste, keeping in mind that the lemon sorbet will also add sweetness. Top up still water.
4. Pour into tumblers and add one or two scoops of lemon sorbet to each.
5. Allow the sorbet to melt a little before drinking.

Banana Chocolate Cooler

Friends and family will line up for refills of this delicious blend of flavors created by Filtron, Huntington Beach, California, USA.

INGREDIENTS

- 1 ripe banana, peeled and cut into chunks
- 1 large scoop chocolate ice-cream
- 1 fl. oz. (30ml) cold brew coffee
- 3 fl. oz. (90ml) filtered water
- 1 scoop coffee ice cubes
- Sugar sprinkles and 1 banana slice, for garnish

METHOD

1. Place all the ingredients in a blender and blend until smooth.
2. Serve in a tall glass and garnish with sugar sprinkles and a banana slice.

Chocolate Malt

This is a classic favorite with chocolate lovers from the days of the drive-in roadside cafe.

INGREDIENTS

- 1 part soft chocolate ice cream
- 3 parts whole milk, well chilled
- 1 generous squeeze chocolate syrup
- 2 large spoons malt powder
- Chocolate vermicelli, for garnish

METHOD

1. Place all the ingredients into a blender and blend until smooth.
2. Pour into a tall glass, sprinkle with chocolate vermicelli, and serve with a thick straw.

Frappé Coffee

This is an easy drink to prepare in batches for family events or parties. You can adjust the drink based on the ice cream you like. Try a traditional vanilla or mix it up with something like raspberry or caramel swirl.

INGREDIENTS

- 8 fl. oz. (240ml) chilled double-strength coffee
- 1 large scoop flavored ice cream
- 1 Tbsp. (15ml) vanilla extract or syrup

METHOD

1. Place all ingredients in a blender and blend the mixture until smooth
2. Serve in a tall glass and garnish with a colorful straw.

Ice Espresso

This creation from Fritz Storm, World Champion Barista 2002, Denmark, tastes like candy and is a great way to end any meal. **Note:** for this recipe you will need a whipped cream siphon that can handle two gas cartridges.

INGREDIENTS

- 1 large scoop vanilla ice cream
- 1 or 2 espressos
- Whipped cream, for garnish

METHOD

1. Melt the ice cream and put it into the whipped cream siphon. Add two gas cartridges. This will change the ice cream to the consistency you would normally have in whipped cream.
2. Make the amount of espresso you'd prefer.
3. Put a little mountain of ice cream from the siphon on top of the espresso.
4. Top with a small amount of whipped cream, if desired.

Frappé Mocha

This drink is like the Frappé Coffee, but comes with a chocolate twist. This is a crowd pleaser that no one turns down and you can have as much fun making it as you will drinking it.

INGREDIENTS

- 8 fl. oz. (240ml) chilled double-strength coffee
- 2 scoops chocolate ice cream
- 1 fl. oz. (30ml) chocolate syrup
- Chocolate shavings, cherries, and a chocolate cookie straw, for garnish

METHOD

1. Place all the ingredients in a blender and blend until smooth.
2. Pour into chilled tall glasses and garnish as desired with chocolate shavings, a cherry, and a chocolate cookie straw.

Mocha Mint Frappé

You can make the cold brew coffee in advance and keep it fresh in the refrigerator. For a similar beverage with less dessert sweetness, enjoy freshly prepared espresso spiked with the freshness of mint.

INGREDIENTS

- 1 cup (240ml) cold brew coffee
- 1 large scoop chocolate ice cream
- 1 fl. oz. (30ml) mint syrup
- Chocolate shavings and a mint sprig, for garnish

METHOD

1. Place all the ingredients in a blender and blend until smooth.
2. Pour the mixture into a tall glass and garnish with chocolate shavings and a mint sprig.

Hazelnut Granita

A perfect dessert of glacé coffee, this recipe from Filtron, Huntington Beach, CA, USA, is as refreshing as it is satisfying. Bring out the cocktail shaker and get into the swing of things. Serve with small chocolates for an elegant final touch.

INGREDIENTS

- 4 fl. oz. (120ml) hazelnut syrup
- 2 fl. oz. (60ml) cold brew coffee or espresso
- 6 fl. oz. (180ml) filtered water
- 2 scoops coffee ice cubes

METHOD

1. Add all the ingredients to a cocktail shaker and shake for 45 seconds.
2. Serve in a chilled glass.

Darling

This very sweet and attractive drink falls somewhere between being a mocktail and a dessert. It's a treat for anybody with a sweet tooth.

INGREDIENTS

- 1 part cherry-flavored syrup
- 1 part sweetened condensed milk
- 1 scoop vanilla ice cream
- Soda water
- 1 scoop raspberry ice cream
- Whipped cream and pineapple chunks, for garnish

METHOD

1. Pour the cherry syrup and condensed milk into a tall glass and mix together.
2. Carefully add the vanilla ice cream, then add soda water to fill about two-thirds of the glass.
3. Now top with a scoop of raspberry ice cream and decorate with a dollop of whipped cream and pineapple chunks.
4. Serve with a thick straw and long-handled spoon.

Choc-nut Sundae Sipper

Chocolate and peanut butter make a beautiful pair and this creamy dessert drink is guaranteed to be a favorite with your friends and family.

INGREDIENTS

- 1 large spoon crunchy peanut butter
- 1 large spoon chocolate syrup
- About 1 cup (240ml) whole milk
- 2 scoops chocolate or pecan ice cream
- Whipped cream and chopped nuts, for garnish

METHOD

1. Place the peanut butter, chocolate syrup, and a little milk into a blender and blend until smooth.
2. Add the remaining milk and the ice cream and blend again for three to four seconds.
3. Pour into a tall glass, top with a dollop of whipped cream, and sprinkle with chopped nuts.

Espresso Malt

Melt the chocolate to the rim of the glass and use a toothpick to create designs. It's artistic, easy, and fun. This delicious soda fountain throwback was created by Stefanie Raymond of Barista's Daily Grind, Kearny, Nebraska, USA.

INGREDIENTS

- 2 fl. oz. (60ml) vanilla syrup
- 1 Tbsp. (15ml) vanilla extract
- 5 fl. oz. (150ml) vanilla ice cream
- 3 Tbsp. (54g) malt powder
- 2 fl. oz. (60ml) espresso

METHOD

1. Place all ingredients in a blender and blend until smooth.
2. Pour the mixture into a tall glass and garnish with a colorful straw and a tall spoon.

Sweet Banana Frappé

Imagine banana, chocolate, and coffee blended to create an elixir that most can't resist.

INGREDIENTS

- 2 cups (480ml) chilled cold brew coffee
- 1 large scoop chocolate ice cream
- 1 ripe banana
- Chocolate shavings, for garnish

METHOD

1. Place all the ingredients in a blender and blend until smooth.
2. Pour into a tall glass and garnish with chocolate shavings.

Popular Cocktail Equivalents

Most of the drinks in this book are original recipes rather than drinks directly inspired by cocktails. The following recipes, however, are alcohol-free versions of well-known, popular cocktails. The alcohol in these drinks is replaced with alcohol-free spirits or ingredients with similar flavors.

Bellini	VeryVery Berry Bellini—48
Bloody Mary	Virgin Mary—76
Buck's Fizz/Mimosa	Baby Buck—81
Colada	Strawberry Colada—84 Virgin Piña Colada—82
Daiquiri	Strawberry Daiquiri—78
Fuzzy Navel	Unfuzzy Navel—76
Horse's Neck	Pony's Neck—88
Manhattan	I'll Fake Manhattan—72
Margarita	Non-Alcoholic Margarita—42 Virgin Margarita—73
Martini	Absentini—45 Fennel Raspberry Martini—69 Iced Flavored Coffee Martini—160
Michelada	What, Me Worry?—72
Mint Julep	Southern Belle—118
Mule	Monday Whiskey Mule—39
Old Fashioned	Maple Bourbon Old Fashioned—62 Mocktail Club's Blackberry "Bold" Fashioned—52
Paloma	Chile Pomegranate Paloma—46
Penicillin	Booze-Free Penicillin—55
San Francisco	San Francisco—78
Sangria	Fun-Gria—80
Sea Breeze	Virgin Sea Breeze—74
Sex on the Beach	Safe Sex on the Beach—75
Southside	Southside Cocktail—68
Ward 8	Ward 8 Cocktail—49
Whiskey Sour	Blackberry Whiskey Sour—38 Spiritless Whiskey Sour—58

Index